MW00827106

TIBETAN MANDALAS, ARTS AND TRADITIONS

TIBETAN MANDALAS, ARTS AND TRADITIONS

CULTURAL AND SPIRITUAL HERITAGE FROM THE HIMALAYAS

PUBLISHED BY CUCO AZUL BOOKS

FIRST EDITION

PUBLISHED BY CUCO AZUL BOOKS

www.cucoazul.org

TABLE OF CONTENTS

PREFACE

Khenpo Tenpa Yungdrung

Bon: The Most Ancient Spiritual Tradition of Tibet

Bon is Tibet's most ancient spiritual and metaphysical tradition, with a profound and far-reaching presence that extends beyond the Tibetan Plateau and into the borderlands of China and Central Asia, as well as into the Himalayan regions of India, Nepal, Sikkim and Bhutan. The founder of our tradition was Tönpa 'the Teacher' Shenrab Miwo, who taught the Bon's numerous systems in a land referred to as Zhangzhung, which included Western Tibet. The teachings were originally in Zhangzhung, a now-vanished language that was closely related to those still spoken in parts of the western Himalayas. According to the historical accounts of Bon, the teachings were subsequently translated into Tibetan during the time of the second Tibetan king, Mutri Tsenpo. The corpus was later expanded with an abundance of commentaries and other writings, producing the thousands of works that make up the corpus of our tradition. In spite of this voluminous literary heritage, not to mention the collected works of many generations of scholars, many misunderstandings about Bon continue to be perpetuated both in Tibet and in the West. However, thanks to several recently established centres in Europe and America, where Tibetan Bon masters provide authentic instruction in their tradition, as well as the growing body of research by members of the international community of scholars, reliable information about Bon is now becoming more readily available. It is in the hope of furthering this understanding of Bon in Europe and the West that we are very happy to present this collection of mandalas, painted according to instructions set forth by the Teacher Shenrab Miwo, and preserved in the ancient scriptures of our tradition.

Khenpo Tenpa Yungdrung
Abbot of the Triten Norbutse Monastery, Kathmandu and Chapter member of Shenten Dargye Ling,Blou, France. Head of Sherig Phuntsok Ling Bön Society, Siliguri, India

©Christophe Moulin

INTRODUCTION

Charles Ramble

Mandalas: Wholeness, Integrity and Perfection

The Sanskrit word *mandala* and the corresponding Tibetan term *kyingkor* both mean "circle;" and, in essence, this is exactly what a mandala is—but with all the deceptive simplicity of the English word itself. The mandala is an ancient and potent symbol found in different forms in numerous Asian metaphysical systems, such as Hinduism, Buddhism and, as in the case of the present collection, Bon. Inasmuch as it is a circle, the mandala has associations of boundedness—something set apart from what lies beyond its perimeter—wholeness, integrity and perfection, and it may represent all these things in different contexts. However, the Tibetan word, which is based on one possible interpretation of the Sanskrit, contains a clue to the most sophisticated application of the motif. *Kyingkor* literally means "centre [and] circle," implying an intimate relationship between core and periphery. And indeed, the practice of the mandala entails one of the most complex and rigorous systems of mental technology ever developed; it was in recognition of this function that no less an authority than the great scholar Giuseppe Tucci described the mandala as a "psychocosmogram." But before explaining what is meant by this concept, a few words of introduction need to be said about Bon.

Bon is a cultural system that incorporates all the spiritual, metaphysical, cosmological and so-called folk traditions of Tibet. While variants of many of these components are also found in Buddhism, it is insufficient to say, as several writers have done, that Bon is a local adaptation of Buddhist beliefs and tenets: it has been unequivocally established that much of the borrowing went in the other direction—from Bon to Buddhism—and that a number of important movements developed in Tibet itself and are shared by the two traditions.

gshed dmar spyi 'dul gyi dkyil 'khor ▶
Mandala of the Universal Conqueror,
the Red Destroyer (of haughty spirits)
Acrylic and mineral color on canvas
67 x 67 cm
2013

However, Bon contains many features that are not found in Buddhism and it is this all-encompassing richness that led some to suggest that the word Bon may be cognate with the name Bod, meaning "Tibet."

The enormous range and diversity of the cultural phenomena covered by the umbrella term "Bon" are rendered less daunting by the fact that they are grouped into different sets, known as "vehicles" or "ways." Scholars within the Bon tradition have themselves devised a number of classifications, of which perhaps the best-known scheme is a nine-set model known as the Nine Ways of Bon. While there is insufficient space here to present the components of the Nine Ways in any detail, broadly speaking, the so-called "lower ways" (known as the Ways of Cause) are concerned primarily with control over the natural world and the development of personal discipline, while the "higher" vehicles (the Ways of Result) deal with progressively more abstract concepts and techniques. These systems are sometimes referred to by the name of the region of Tibet in which they were developed. Thus, the mandalas that we see in this exhibition are classified according to a nine-vehicle system known as the "Central Treasures." "Treasures" refers to texts that were concealed to save them from destruction when Bon was persecuted in Central Tibet (hence "Central") in the eighth century and brought to light again at a more propitious time. The mandalas are drawn and painted according to the precise iconometric prescriptions set out in the Fifth to the Eighth Ways. The names of these vehicles are as follows:

1. The Way of Primordial Bon Purifying Activities
2. The Way of Miraculous Power of Many Sorts
3. The Way of the Playfulness of Compassion Producing Real Results
4. The Way of Completion Endowed with Supreme Profits

An important principle of Bon is that the self is an illusion, created by a configuration of cosmic aggregates that are given local and individual form through the displacement of the mind from the essence of the mind. This essence, by contrast, is neither local nor individual, but universal, transcending consciousness and associated with the infinity of space. T.S. Eliot once remarked that: "Humankind cannot bear very much reality." The great Bon masters were keenly aware of this fact, understanding that the task of uniting the

pad ma klong yangs kyi dkyil 'khor
Mandala of the (pure) Lotus of the Open Expanse
Acrylic and mineral color on canvas
86 x 86 cm
2013

mind with its own essence requires the use of abstractions that would be far beyond the capacities of even relatively advanced practitioners. The "psychocosmographic" mandala was a highly effective device that was developed for this precise purpose. The mandala model of the 'centre-and-circle' can stand for the individual human being, or it can stand for the entire universe; this is precisely the point. The abstract energies of human potential and of the cosmos itself are rendered accessible to the practitioner by being represented, according to iconographic conventions, as partially anthropomorphic figures with attributes that can be understood by anyone schooled in those conventions. The student dedicates long periods to memorising and absorbing the geometry of the complex diagram and learning by heart the explanatory texts that underlie it. Eventually he or she will have internalised it to a degree where the whole configuration and the visual support (and "support" is, in fact, a literal translation of the Tibetan term) can be generated internally, through concentrated visualisation. "Generation" is a crucial phase of mandala technology. Like the universe itself, the mandala is produced from the void, and for this purpose, the student visualises the void—far more easily said than done, of course!—and, in that void, the appearance of a single point that is itself the product of imagined sensory phenomena, including sounds, colours and shapes. From this point, the practitioner "generates" the universe in a microcosmic equivalent of the Big Bang, with geometric order unfolding all around the centre, according to the specifications of the mandala that has been so thoroughly internalised. The individual is unconstrained by the notion of "self," the mind is unbounded, and the generated mandala extends beyond the confines of personhood to identification with thecosmos itself.

The practitioner then proceeds to gather the entire creation back into the centre in the second phase of the technique, known as "completion." The culmination of this phase is the realisation of the contingency of all phenomena, and the union of awareness with space. The technique is one that has been tested and refined over many generations, and the procedure is intensely practical during the preliminary training.

dus kyi 'khor lo'i dkyil 'khor ▶
Kalachakra Mandala, the wheel of time.
Acrylic and mineral color on canvas
86 x 86 cm
2013

khro bo smug nag 'khyil ba'i dkyil 'khor
Mandala of the Radiating Dark Brown Wrathful (deity)
Acrylic and mineral color on canvas
67 x 67 cm
2013

The mandala technology represented by each of the ways contained in this collection reflects this principle of incremental development. In the case of the first group (corresponding to the Fifth Way), the practitioner cultivates an attitude of cautious respect for the energetic core, instilling the critical understanding that this is not a trivial activity to be taken lightly, and that the tried and tested procedures must be observed if this course of mental gymnastics is to have beneficial, rather than destructive, results. The second group—the Sixth Way—sees the practitioner developing an easy intimacy with this powerful core. The third entails full identification with the centre, and the implementation of the "generation" process outlined above, while the Eighth Way is marked by the fusion of the practitioner's awareness with the infinity of space, and the concluding process of "Completion" or "Perfection." The sixteen mandalas in this collection are a unique set painted by one of the finest artists currently working in the Bon tradition. Followers of Bon account for only about one-tenth of the population of Tibet.

The cultural pressures faced by all Tibetans in their own homeland, coupled with the flight of so many Tibetans to other countries, puts the integrity of the entire Bon culture at risk. The monastic tradition of Bon is flourishing, but Bon is far more than a religion in the narrow sense of the word; it requires an environment that brings together the linguistic, cultural, artistic and technological components of its heritage. The plan to develop such an educational centre is currently being implemented under the guidance of Khenpo Tenpa Yungdrung on the border of India and Nepal, where land has been acquired and construction work is underway. The cost of such an enterprise is considerable, and it is intended that all the proceeds from the sale of the mandalas exhibited here should be directed to the creation of this centre, to help sustain the very tradition that produced them: a tradition that was born and flourished on the high Tibetan Plateau, but has a special relevance to the modern world as a treasured part of the common heritage of mankind.

Charles Ramble
Ecole Pratique des Hautes Etudes,
Sciences Historiques et Philologiques
Paris, France

ART EXHIBITIONS FOR BUILDING A SCHOOL IN INDIA

Mara Arizaga and Ioana Creitaru (Editors)

Due to the isolation and remoteness of its communities, the Himalayan region has preserved several distinct varieties of autochthonous knowledge and culture. This includes one traditional form of art, Mandala painting.

Rich with symbolism, each mandala included in this collection and reproduced in the present catalogue portrays several features of Tibetan culture, as well as the variety of factors that influenced it over the centuries, particularly those of the Bon tradition.

Taken as a whole, Himalayan art plays an essential role in preserving and passing to new generations the symbolic dialogue between spiritual traditions and their followers. The sacred images contained in most forms of Himalayan art are not only important for their spiritual and moral functions, but also serve as valuable repositories of Himalayan artistic customs.

In line with EVA's main objectives, the *"Mandalas: Mirrors of the Cosmos"* exhibition, first displayed at the Bel-Air Fine Art Gallery in Geneva and later at l'Espace Lhomond in Paris, aims to raise awareness of this valuable Himalayan legacy and to promote Himalayan customs, artistic skills, and cultural values in Europe and beyond. It also aims to support EVA's project on the Tise Himalayan International School (THIS) in Siliguri, India.

This expanded version of the original exhibition catalogue includes contributions from renowned authors and experts in the Himalayan cultural traditions, including on Tibetan medicine, sacred landscapes, and the modern use of ancient Himalayan practices.

This book includes rich paintings, both in *thangkas* (Tibetan Buddhist or Bon paintings) and in stories that relate the journeys of treasure discoverers and revealers. It explores Tibetan medicine and the potential contemporary applications of Tibetan practices to understand how the rich culture of Bon can interact with today's world.

This volume also includes a *thangka* portraying the figure of Shenchen Luga, a Bon "terton," which is a term used to describe a discoverer of ancient hidden Buddhist or Bonpo texts. Samten Karmey sheds light into this particularly prominent historic character from the Yungdrung religion, who is said to have lived in Tibet at the beginning

©Leva Rute

©Courtesy of Khenpo Tenpa Yungdrung

of the 11th century, and is believed to have excavated ancient manuscripts with many of the teachings of Bon. Karmay delves into the different elements of the painting, and explains its importance and lasting relevance.

A further *thangka* painting is explored by Marietta Kind Furger, showing the life of an accomplished Bon master, Treton Namkha Gyaltsen, who is thought to have lived from the late 17th century to the early 18th century. Kind's article examines aspects of his biography and the struggles that he faced.

The art of this book is complemented by a poem by Tenzin Wangyal Rinpoche, in which grief for the 2015 earthquake that hit Nepal weighs heavy. Rinpoche's poem beautifully captures the tragedy of the innocent people who died, and carves out a lasting sense of loss and pain, followed by a prayer for the world.

Next, Katia Buffetrille delves into the importance of mandalas to the Bon religion, exploring the concept of "ideal mandalas," which are projected onto specific landscapes, and the role of territorial or mountain gods to the Bon religion.

This journey through art and history is expanded upon by Francoise Pommaret, who brings the reader to Bhutan. Here, she briefly discusses two temples that are linked to another terton, named Dorje Lingpa (1346-1405). Dorje Lingpa was both Bon (with the name *Bon zhig gling pa or gYung drung gling pa*) and Buddhist, and Pommaret masterfully uncovers his life in the Shar region (now the district of Wangdu Phodrang) in the west of Bhutan, followed by his journey to Bumthang in Central Bhutan.

Stepping into the present, Alejandro Chaoul shares information about how Himalayan traditions are beginning to filter into contemporary western settings. He looks as the ways in which mind-body practices, particularly Tibetan Bon Yoga of Channels-breath (*rTsa rLung*) and Magical movements (*'Phrul 'Khor*), can complement and aid modern western cultures, and how these have traditionally been practiced in Tibet and in the Himalayas.

Subsequently, the book travels to examine two ancient and significant rock paintings. Both depict Tapihritsa, a key figure from the Yungdrung Bon tradition. John Vincent Bellezza reveals why these paintings are key to understanding the history of the tradition, and what their significance is today.

The book next explores the Bon *mendrub* ritual, which aims to transform medicinal powder with 120 ingredients into an exceptionally potent medicine, believed to be able to cure the 400 classes of diseases that are mentioned in Tibetan medicine. The *mendrub* ritual is complex and requires a great deal of preparation and dedication, so insights into its intricacies are rare.

Finally, the book aims to offer a summary of how the Himalayan and Tibetan arts, traditions, and practices are still living and breathing in today's world, and how crucial it is that we continue to protect them. It acknowledges their history and their future, and offers sincere respect and reverence to the diverse and rich elements of the Himalayan culture.

Mara Arizaga and Ioana Creitaru (Editors)

stag la bdag rdzogs kyi dkyil 'khor
Mandala of the Self Perfected (deity) Tagla
Acrylic and mineral color on canvas
86 x 86 cm
2013

A PAINTING OF BONPO MASTERS BY KHYUNGPO YUNGDRUNG GYALTSEN

Samten G. Karmay

Samten G. Karmay

This is a *thangka* that contains images of some historical figures of the Bon tradition. In its composition, it is a unique painting, for it depicts the figure of Shenchen Luga (Fig.1), who may be described as the promulgator of Yungdrung Bon, the Bon religion, in Tibet, at the beginning of the 11th century. The painting includes some of his prominent pupils, who belonged to families such as Dru and Zhu. These families lived in different parts of Tsang, Central Tibet. There are also images of early Bonpo masters (Fig. 2, 3, 4, 7) as well as well as images of some masters from Amdo.

The Bon tradition maintains that Shenchen Luga excavated old manuscripts in Digtsam Thakar in Tsang. These manuscripts contained various teachings regarded as valuable for spiritual attainment. His assembled manuscripts came to form the core of the Bon canon.

The other spiritual masters depicted in the painting (Fig. 2, 3, 4, 7) were not directly connected with Shenchen Luga, but they played very important roles in the development of Shenchen Luga's teachings.

Fig.1 Shenchen Luga (996-1035).

Fig.2 Gyermi Nyiwo. This master was a yogin and is believed to have lived in the 12th century.

Fig.3 Maton Sroldzin (b.1092) was a master who revealed many hidden religious manuscripts.

Fig.4 Yilton Ponse Khyunggotsal (b.1175) was a master who also revealed hidden manuscripts.

Fig.5 Druchen Namkha Yungdrung of the Dru family was a disciple of Shenchen Luga. He took care of his master's philosophical manuscripts.

Fig.6 Gyalse Shuye Legpo of the Shu family was a very close disciple of Shenchen Luga. He followed the teachings on Dzogchen meditation. These two pupils, Dru and Shu, eventually returned to their own homes and established religious centres.

Fig.7 Meu Lhari Nyenpo (1024-1091) of the Meu family, an important master of the teachings left behind by Shenchen Luga. More detailed stories of master Shenchen Luga and his pupils can be found in Samten G. Karmay, "A Historical Overview of the Bon Religion" (Samten Karmay, Jeff Watt, T*he Magic Word, The Indigenous Religion of Tibet,* Rubin Museum of Art, New York, Philip Wilson Publishers, London 2007, pp.55-81).

Fig.8 Kyangtrul Lungtog Kalzang Gyatsho (20th century). He belongs to the Kyangtrul lineage in Phenchu, Amdo.

Fig.9 Bongya Rangshar Rangdrol.

Fig.10 Bongya Yungdrung Phuntshog.

Fig.11 Bongya Namkha Gyalstshen.

These three Bongya masters belong to the Bongya lineage in Rebkong, Amdo, and lived in the 19th and 20th centuries.

The painter Khyungpo Yungdrung Gyaltsen presently lives in Rebkong, Amdo.

This *thangka* was published by National Museum of Ethnology (Tsumagari, S. & Tachikawa, M., (2011). *Bonpo Thangkas from Rebkong.*

gshed dmar spyi 'dul gyi dkyil 'khor ▶
Mandala of the Universal Conqueror,
the Red Destroyer (of haughty spirits)
Acrylic and mineral color on canvas
67 x 67 cm
2013

BIOGRAPHICAL THANGKA **ON THE LIFE OF TRETON NAMKHA GYALTSEN FROM DOLPO (NEPAL)**

Marietta Kind Furger

Marietta Kind Furger

The *thangka* describes major events in the life of Treton Namkha Gyaltsen from Pugmo, who spent most of his life in solitary retreats in the surrounding area, where he composed numerous songs. His biography became an important part of the local history. It is annually performed in public in Pugmo and Tsho villages during the major village ritual, the Matri Puja, in the form of a duet between the lamas and the villagers. The lamas read the texts and sing the songs. After every two lines of song, the villagers answer by reciting the Matri *mantra (Om matri muye sale du)*. The performance continues day and night and the songs regularly cause people to cry with joy and devotion.

The autobiography of Treton Namkha Gyaltsen, who is thought to have lived from the late 17th century to the early 18th century, is written in Tibetan cursive script and consists of ninety-eight folios. It is written in a pleasant style and it speaks of the practitioner's progress in ritual practices as well as his doubts and difficulties. In several sections, he presents his thoughts and teachings in the form of songs.

This painting by *thangka* painter Yungdrung Yeshe from Pugmo was inspired by Treton Namkha Gyaltsen's biography. The image at the bottom corner of the thangka describes a dream of Treton Namkha Gyaltsen that had strongly influenced him. It is about his encounter with the Lord of Death and his narrow escape from the stay in hell. This dream, in combination with another dream of his encounter with the great teacher Tonpa Sherab Miwo and the accounts of his great forefather Treton Bonnyi Zangpo, who attained the rainbow body, caused his deep interest in Yungdrung Bon religion. At the age of thirteen, he left home to join his paternal uncle, Treton Monlam Gyaltsen, at their monastic seat in Merphu, near Do-Tarap, where he received his first initiation and took the decision to dedicate his life to religion. After various solitary retreats, he came back to Pugmo for the Dzogchen teachings of Treton Bonnyi Gyaltsen.

Painter: Yungdrung Yeshe of Khyungpo, *sertsa* lineage from Pugmo. Painted in: 1998

At twenty-three, he finally took his novice monk vows. Since his family had no male heir, he was asked to get married, but refused. Instead he retired to the Pumer monastery and later to the great solitary place of Lama Chumik (*Bla ma chu mig*), the "Holy Spring Created by the Lama," a cliff overhang with a sacred spring of his forefather Treton Nyima Senge. This scene can be seen at the top left corner of the *thangka*.

After his three-year retreat at Lama Chumik, the villagers arrived to celebrate his accomplishments with countless presents. However, Treton Namkha Gyaltsen decided to add another nine years in retreat in the valley of Gungthang. He stayed a little bit further down, at the cave hermitage called Shugrinyishar (*Shug ri nyi shar*, meaning "The Mountain Site where the Rising Sun shines through the Juniper Tree") and later nearby in a small dwelling called Säkhang, that his sister built for him. Visitors and other distracting activities led to the decline of his virtuous accomplishments and he gave way to some sort of wavering. In order to focus again on the thoughts of enlightenment, he started to sing a number of songs of encouragement to himself and contemplated impermanence. At times, he felt so lonely that he started to talk with the snow grouse (upper middle right of the *thangka*). In another section, he describes his inner conflicts, wherein his body and his mind struggle with one another and move in different directions, causing him trouble. His "self-originated awareness" was sitting in judgement over this dispute and tried to bring them into harmony, because all three are of interdependent origin.

After his nine years of retreat, he took the *gelong* vows, the highest ordination of a Bon monk, from Yangton Tsultrim Namgyal, and received further initiations and teachings. For the rest of his life, he mainly stayed in the above-mentioned hermitages, where he started to teach more extensively (middle lower left of the *thangka*). He gave many teachings in the form of songs. When he grew old, he also sang about the weakening of his body and, once more, his body and mind started to argue. When he passed away, he remained for three days in an upright position (*thugs dam*) until his body burned by itself, accompanied by a great number of auspicious signs and leaving behind many relics.

For more detail on the biography, please refer to:

Kind, M. (2012). The Bon Landscape of Dolpo – Pilgrimages, Monasteries, Biographies and the Emergence of Bon. Bern, Switzerland: Peter Lang Verlag.

khro bo smug nag 'khyil ba'i dkyil 'khor ▶
Mandala of the Radiating Dark Brown Wrathful (deity)
Acrylic and mineral color on canvas
67 x 67 cm
2013

ཁྲོ་བོ་སྔགས་རྣམས་འཁྱིལ་བའི་དཀྱིལ་འཁོར།།

FROM A LAMENTING HEART

Tenzin Wangyal Rinpoche

A Spontaneous Poem

by Tenzin Wangyal Rinpoche, May 10, 2015

While teaching the Bon in Spain
I hear the news of an earthquake in Nepal.
Instantly the hairs on my body stand up
Sadness whirls in my heart
Anguish penetrates my body.

Is this the punishment of angry local deities?
Or natural, *samsaric* destruction?
Or simply a fate that has befallen us?
Beneath the earth, stones collide.
There can be no certainty of any reason.
A profusion of causes and conditions
In spaces outer, inner, and secret
Result in this elemental dream-like disaster.
Among the thousands of dead and injured
Men and women, children and elderly.
Mother and child, once inseparable even for a moment,
Now apart, forever.
How appalling.
Couples bonded in love and affection,
With dreams for a lifetime together,
Are torn apart and permanently separated.
My heart fills with agony.

In any family, many are dead.
Some are left alive and injured.
All that had been earned is lost.
All that had been built up has collapsed.
Lonely, friendless, hopeless, exhausted,
A survivor looks to the sky and sees only a void,
Looks down at a collapsed wall and sees corpses.
Minds wander untethered like souls between lives.
Fathers, spent of strength, do not know what to do.
Grandparents nearing the completion of contented lives
Once full of children and grand-
children leading joyful lives
Are now alone.
A home with generations of memories—gone.
Spiritual monuments, priceless objects of heritage
Turned to rubble in a moment.
I am pierced with sadness.

There is a thundering sorrow beneath the earth.
Who listens? No one.
The sound vanishes like an echo.
An innocent newborn child,
Who has not even seen the light of this world,
Experiences life and death at once.

Challenging even to imagine.
Like a bad omen in a dream
This too will dissolve.
People will gradually forget.
One day, it will be difficult to trace what happened here.

Therefore, in this crucial time, let us remember!
The deceased of Nepal and Tibet have
a long history of friendship.
Let us perform a dedication prayer and join our merit.
All who survive—laity, monks, and nuns
United in heartfelt sadness
Can lift some load of suffering, whether small or large.
Each of us can dispel another's dark-
ness with the light of compassion.
Each of us can bear witness to the grieving of another.
When we have lost the way for-
ward and do not know what to do,
When we cannot see the light because
of the darkness of suffering,
At that moment, our advice to
one another is precious.
To intelligent men and women,
There is no greater demonstra-
tion of impermanence than this.
Now have the diligence to understand!
Old and young are liable to become sick.
The circumstances of your own death are uncertain.
Possibly, your death is very close.

Do not concern yourself with elabo-
rate strategies for this lifetime.
Do not abandon your peace to busyness.
Do not abandon your happiness in pursuit of wealth.
Do not abandon your compassion in anger.

As if there were just today to live,
Do good for yourself and others.
Enjoy close friends and family.
Learn a new art form to be wiser.
Laugh like a child thousands
upon thousands of times.
Take joy in activities outside your profession.
Even if one finds true happiness in that
which is considered crazy, do it!
Spread your love and compassion
like the million rays of the sun.
An altruistic heart effortlessly works for good.
Turn your happiness like a wheel—in all directions.
Endeavour to work without bias
for all beings and for truth.

This earthquake is a master of appearance.
If you still have difficulty understand-
ing the essence of the teachings
After a lifetime of listening,
Perhaps now your heart has been moved.
If your mind is still unripe

After completing nine hundred thousand preliminary practices,
Perhaps now your mind has been tamed.
I praise the masters of natural existence!

For these deceased and faultless people,
With compassion and respect from the core of my heart
I will offer these strings of words like necklaces of flowers.
Every time I pray, I will not forget.
I dedicate my virtuous actions to all who suffer.
May you be liberated in a pure land.

This is a spontaneous poem written by Ababa (Tenzin Wangyal Rinpoche) in Berlin, Germany in 2015. Translated from Tibetan to English by Dr. Sangmo Yangri and Matthew Conover. Edited by Marcy Vaughn.

dbal mo srid pa spyi 'dul gyi dkyil 'khor ▶
Mandala of Walmo Sidpa Chidul; The Fierce Female Conqueror of the Whole Universe
Acrylic and mineral color on canvas
67 x 67 cm
2013

THE MANDALA LANDSCAPE

Katia Buffetrille

Katia Buffetrille

Ecole Pratique des Hautes Etudes,
Centre de recherche sur les civilisations de l'Asie orientale, Paris

The *mandalas* shown in this exhibition are not only visual representations of the dwelling of a Buddha and his assembly, but also meditation tools. They are drawn as square-shaped palaces with four doors, facing the four cardinal directions, and inscribed within a circle. The *mandala* is positioned with east facing down, south to the left, west above, and north to the right. This type of *mandala* has served as the archetype for the ideal city, also as a model for the cosmos, a blueprint for sacred architecture and a diagram for the distribution of vital energies inside the human body.

However, the *mandala* concept is also linked to some Tibetan landscapes, a result of the interaction between indigenous religious beliefs and Buddhism, which was brought to Tibet in the 7th century.

This article does not focus on *mandalas* similar to those presented in this exhibition, but on a different type: the ideal *mandala*, projected on a landscape by a process that some have described as "mandalisation." This is the landscape of the sacred mountains.

1. Monks creating a sand mandala.
Tawang Monastery (India, Arunachal Pradesh),
2011 © Katia Buffetrille

Tibetan Sacred Mountains

The way Tibetans depict mountains and the functions they have attributed to them have changed over the centuries, but the mountains remain as important as ever.

Long before Buddhism was introduced into Tibet (7th century), mountains were a key element of the landscape, not just as a physical element, but also as an indestructible and ancient religious substratum. According to indigenous beliefs, the gods of heaven, *Chya*, are considered to be mountains of heaven, creators of the world. They sent some of their own to Earth so that "the sky is stretched above the earth, at the very top, without crumbling and the earth down does not collapse."

The king, regarded as the son of these mountain-gods, plays a central role on earth. His divine status justifies his authority, as well as the hierarchical divisions of the society. Moreover, he has a special relationship with the natural environment because the mountain-gods are the source of life-giving water, which the monarch controls.

The first divine kings, celestial gods sent to Earth, were expected to re-enact the descent of the first king to Tibet, a "high

2. King Songtsen Gampo's tomb (7th century), Valley of Yarlung, Central Tibet, 1987 © Katia Buffetrille

country, land of purity." While they stayed on earth during the day, they were thought to return to heaven – temporarily at night and permanently at the time of their death. To this end, they used a rainbow-coloured rope, the *mu* rope, which linked their sinciput to heaven and in which their bodies was said to dissolve. This rope is sometimes identified with the mountain or the "celestial ladder" from which the first king descended on earth. According to tradition, only the first seven kings used it. Grigum, the 8th monarch, cut it by mistake in a duel that pitted him against one of his subjects. From that time on, the kings, in spite of their divine nature, have left their bodies on Earth. This led to the first royal funerary rites and the construction of tombs.

The idea of ladder or rope was never completely forgotten, although nowadays it's hiding under a layer of Buddhist traditions. One can still see ladders painted on the cliffs towering above some roads in Central Tibet. These ladders are drawn to help the dead break free from the cycle of rebirth (*samsâra*) in order to reach the ultimate fulfilment of enlightenment.

3. Ladders painted on cliffs, not far from Lhasa, 2010 © Katia Buffetrille

The *kulas* were very important deities in ancient times. These *kulas*, whose worship is attributed to the first king, were thought to be both sacred mountains and ancestors. They were essentially the gods of the ruling class and were seen as the foundation on which the vital principles of the ruler and various lords rested. However, their worship concerned the whole population, for, if displeased, the *kulas* guaranteed neither the stability, nor the prosperity of the kingdom; they could even abandon the monarch or the lords, leading to their deaths. But if they were correctly propitiated, they assured the king and local chiefs of their protection. To this end, seasonal ceremonies, including offerings, libations and animal sacrifices, were dedicated to them in summer and winter alike.

The importance of these mountain-gods related to the monarchy gradually declined, probably due to the conversion of kings to Buddhism. *Kula* worship seems to have totally disappeared in Tibet under this name, but the term has not been forgotten and continues to exist in the names of mountains such as Kula Gangri, a mountain on the border of Bhutan and Tibet.

4. The Kula Gangri Mountain,
Southern Tibet, 1986 © Katia Buffetrille

The worship of mountain-deities has survived in the cult of the "territorial gods" (*yüllha*). This mountain-god, master of a given territory, is considered to be the mythical ancestor of both the territory and the population living on it, as indicated by the term *amnye* (ancestor) that often appears in his name: for example in Amnye Machen,

▲
5. The Amnye Machen Mountain in Amdo,
1990 © Katia Buffetrille

the most important sacred mountain of Amdo, north-eastern region of Tibet, or Amnye Nyenchen, a mountain to the northeast of Labrang monastery, one of the great monasteries of the gelug school, also in Amdo.

Local lore sometimes explicitly links the origin of clans to the "territorial god:" according to legend, the god Nyenpo Yutse, identified with a mountain on the Upper Yellow River, also located in Amdo, gave his daughter in marriage to a human to thank him for having saved his son, who had been abducted by a falcon. Their union begat three sons, from whom are said to descend three tribes of Golok nomads living near the mountain.

Tibetans have an anthropomorphic view of the "territorial god:" he is perceived as a human being with virtues and faults. The "territorial god" is happy when he is pleased, for example by being shown feats of strength, courage, as well as by beautiful words, dances, and so on. However, if not honoured in a proper way, he may express his displeasure by causing various disasters. He is generally portrayed as a warrior god (*dralha* or "god who subdues enemies") wearing helmet and armour, and mounted – generally on a horse, but sometimes on a mule or deer.

6. The Nyenpo Yutse Mountain in Amdo,
2011 © Katia Buffetrille

7. The god Amnye Machen, Goge Monastery, Amdo, 2011 © Katia Buffetrille

These gods are usually male, but some are female. The Lalu nomads, who live in Markyang, Western Tibet, have the mountain Jomo Gangkar, "Lady, White Snow Mountain" as their "territorial goddess."

The cult of the "territorial god," a secular and oral custom, was traditionally practised on a daily and annual basis. Long forbidden after the Chinese occupation of the 1950s, it has been revived in some regions of Tibet. Even today, one can frequently see Tibetans making daily offerings of fragrant smoke (*sang*) to their "territorial god" on the terrace roofs of their houses.

Moreover, in some villages, once a year, one man from each family rides to the place of ceremony carrying an arrow. The place is usually located at a pass or at the top of a mountain. The village chief usually carries a longer arrow compared to the other villagers. Once they reach the altar, one of them blows into a conch and they all make a smoke offering of juniper, alcohol and grilled barley flour (*tsampa*). Then they plant their arrows in the square stone or wood structure intended to receive them (*labtse*), among those left from the previous year. They recite an invocation to the "territorial god" and throw up to the sky the paper "wind horses" (*lungta*), each

8. The Jomo Gangkar Mountain, 2000. © Katia Buffetrille

calling upon himself the various riches he hopes to receive. The "territorial god," provider of worldly boons, bestows glory, honour, reputation, wealth, power and fertility to the community inhabiting the territory under his protection. Traditionally, the ritual was followed by various contests: horse racing, rifle shooting, archery. The idea of individual differences was very present, and the purpose of the ritual was to please the god, to perform feats, to show one's physical strength. However, the mountain-gods demanded not only warlike exploits, but also animal sacrifices, a practice in total contradiction with the Buddhist ideal of compassion towards all beings.

10. An Amdowa on his way to worship Taglung Mountain, Amdo, 1997 © Katia Buffetrille

9. Morning sang offering, Kyangtshang, Amdo, 1986 © Katia Buffetrille

▲

11. The cult of ***yüllha:*** *all throw the "wind horses" (lungta),* 1997. © Katia Buffetrille

Buddhist authorities could not accept bloody offerings (*marchö*), nor could they brutally suppress the many rites related to ancient beliefs that had been part of the Tibetan world since the very early times, because they would have met with strong resistance. They started by tackling the issues of rites, while retaining the goals that the native rite wanted to achieve. They transformed a "territorial god" mountain (*yüllha*) into a "Buddhist holy place" mountain (*néri*). New rituals, the main one being the practice of circumambulation, have materialized the Buddhist control on the old practice.

The initial act of this process, which can be named "buddhicisation," is the "opening of the door of the pilgrimage" (*nego chepa*) by a predestined being, who will give all devotees access to the holy place. The victorious Buddhism transforms a local mountain into a mountain of universal scope. The inhabitants of a particular territory may be the only ones allowed to worship their territorial god and to expect from him prosperity, honours, power and other earthly boons, but everyone can honour the sacred Buddhist mountain (*neri*) and expect from the pilgrimage a positive response to spiritual requests, according to their personal achievements.

The pilgrimage guides (*neyig*)

Written sources play a crucial role in the transformation of a "territorial god" mountain (*yüllha*) into a "Buddhist holy place" mountain (*neri*). The pilgrimage guides (neyig) are one of the main vectors of the symbolic appropriation of space. In fact, contrary to what their name might suggest, these works are by no means guides in the sense that we understand them in the West because their function is not to help the pilgrim find his way along the circumambulation path. These writings, which were composed by meditation practitioners or religious scholars, have an ideological purpose. They aim to embed the Buddhist pantheon in the landscape in order to proceed to the symbolic appropriation of a space that was traditionally occupied by deities of the non-Buddhist world.

The descriptions of holy places found in these texts are intended to transcend the pilgrim's thought and to change his view from a landscape filled with traditional beliefs to that of a Buddhist holy place. Therefore, these guides present the mountain in question as the ideal centre of a *mandala* constituted by the whole surrounding landscape. The mountain is then described as the seat of a Buddhist deity (in general, Demchog – a very important tantric deity among the Kagyüpa) and therefore constitutes the deity's palace. It is furthermore identified with the stûpa, the Buddhist monument par excellence, which was built to house relics of Buddha or great saints.

The landscape these guides aim to depict is at the same time symbolic and real. The symbolic landscape makes use of the topography, thus illustrating the supremacy of the spiritual over the temporal. The mountain is generally presented according to two levels of perception: that of the ordinary pilgrim who sees only a snowy mountain, and that of the meditation practitioner who has access to a much subtler level and penetrates the true nature of phenomena. The Tantric master Düdül Dorje (1615-1672), for example, describes the Kawakarpo, sacred mountain of Kham, in these terms:

12. Kawakarpo Mountain, Kham, 2003. © Katia Buffetrille

Externally, it is a snowy mountain formed by one hundred white crystal stupas. Internally, the thousand Buddhas of our cosmic era reside there. One hundred thousand heroes and *dâkinîs* surround it. Saints scatter flowers while singing praises.

The same opposition between the "exterior" and "interior" visions can be found in one of the Amnye Machen pilgrimage guides:

Outwardly, these mountain holy places appear as mounds of dusty earth, but in reality, their essence is that of the paradises arising from the manifestation of wisdom and they are not different from the paradises of the Potala [paradise of Chenrezig] or Riwotse Nga [paradise of Jampelyang].

Kawakarpo (Düdül Dorje) receives the same treatment:

Exoterically, this pilgrimage guide is that of Kawakarpo; esoterically, it is that of the tutelary deity Demchog.

The pilgrimage guides devoted to sacred mountains are based on stereotypes, especially the "submission" of space. Before being Buddhicised, space is considered to be wild. The term "submission" really comes into its own in this case. Tibetans use the verb *dülwa,* which means "to subdue, to subjugate." The aim of Buddhists is not only to "tame" the ego in order to break free from the cycle of existences (*samsara*), but also to "subjugate" the indigenous numina associated with various territories and landscapes in order to make them the protectors of the religion. According to tradition, the soil of the Land of snow had to be tamed to be inhabited: because the territory of Tibet as it was in its imperial extension was occupied by the body of a demoness, lying on her back, (7th-9th centuries), the first king nailed the demoness to the ground by building temples at the four corners of three concentric square areas. Thanks to this civilizing action, Buddhism was able to grow.

In the same way, the subjugation of local deities is the process by which Buddhists transform "wild" spaces into "civilized" ones. The territorial gods, who are non-Buddhist mountains deities, are subdued by great tantric masters, who transform them into protectors of the religion.

Pilgrimage guides also describe the visions meditation practitioners may have, visions in which the landscape is populated with Buddhist deities who supplant local deities. For example, Künga Kewang Pelzangpo, one author of a pilgrimage guide, describes the successive visions he had at Amnye Machen. Among them:

In the centre of this snow mountain called Amnye Machen [...] I saw clearly all the divine assemblies of the glorious Demchog gathered in a divine palace whose intrinsic nature was the spontaneously radiance wisdom of the thought of Demchog [...].[1]

While the ancient beliefs do not seem to distinguish between the "mountain territorial god" and the mountain as "residence of the territorial god," the guides of pilgrimage describe the mountains as residences of divinities. They distinguish between the support (the mountain identified with a *mandala or a stûpa*), and the divinity who resides on it. One might think that a gradual shift has taken place, by means of Buddhist literature, from "mountain deity" to "mountain residence of the deity," the first step towards the notion of "*mandala* palace mountain" of the deity.

But this Buddhicisation is neither a linear, nor a monolithic phenomenon as the comparison of two mountains (Amnye Machen, in Eastern Tibet and Kailash, in Western Tibet) clearly demonstrates.

Kailash went through a particularly successful process of Buddhicisation, as evidenced by the many Buddhist texts devoted to it. The existence of a protector of the soil, Gangri Lhabtsen, of whom we only find very few depictions (I have only seen

1 All translations are from Katia Buffetrille 2000, Pilgrims, Lamas and Visionaries. Oral and written sources on Tibetan pilgrimages, Wiener Studien zur Tibetology und Buddhismuskunde. Heft 46, (Wien, Arbeitskreis für Tibetische und Buddhistische Studien Universität Wien).

13. Mount Kailash, Western Tibet, 1996. © Katia Buffetrille

one), is very rarely mentioned. He appears very pacified: he is depicted as a white deity mounted on a white horse, wearing neither armour, nor weapons.

Just as the main deity of the mandala resides at its centre, the pristine summit of Kailash rises in the heart of a landscape featuring four monasteries marking the four directions: Gyangdrag – "Whose fame extends far and wide;" Choku – "Body of the Law;" Driraphug – "Cave of the female yak horn;" Tsudrül phug – "Cave of magical abilities." Four places of prostration indicate the four directions. All mountains and rocky outcroppings bear the names of Buddhist deities. The 'traces' are many: some were left by the many mystics who meditated in this place, while some feature deities and Buddhist symbols.

There are three paths of circumambulation, each of them intended for a category of beings according to their progress along

14. Gangri Lhabtsen, Purang, Western Tibet, 1996. © Katia Buffetrille

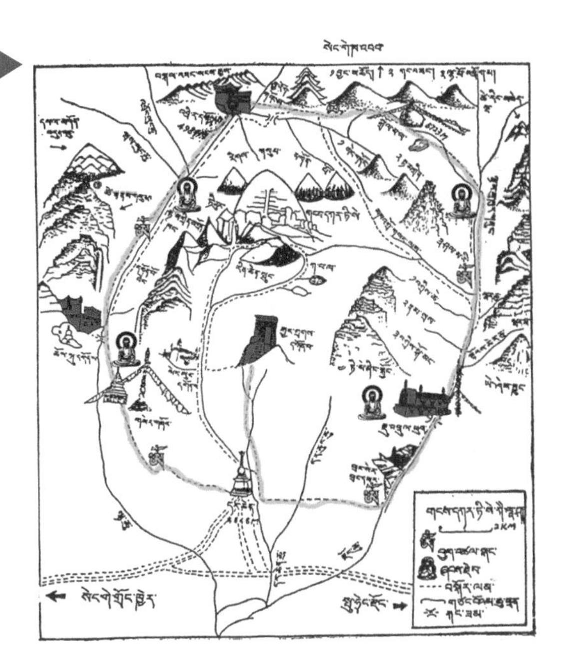

15. Carte du Kailash.
(Bod jlongs nang bstan 1990, n°1)

the path of spiritual elevation: the "outer," which is the longest, reserved for ordinary beings; an "intermediate" one for the *Dakinis*; and the "inner one" for the five hundred *arhats*, the first disciples of Buddha. The existence of three kinds of paths in most holy places is part of the Buddhicisation process, which seeks to institutionalise the pilgrim's progress in the sacred space.

Moreover, one year (horse-year) and one specific date are particularly auspicious for a pilgrimage: the 15th day of the 4th Tibetan month (May-June), the date of Buddha's birth, illumination and death (*parinirvâna*).

Pilgrims come to the Kailash from all parts of Tibet, drawn by the mountain's fame, but also confident that the Buddhist deities who reside there can fulfil their wishes and grant them good rebirths. They approach the holy place on foot, dressed very simply and unarmed. Their main ritual acts consist of circumambulations, prostrations, offerings and recitation of *mantras*, similar to monastery rituals, following the recommendations given by the guides.

16. Buddhist pilgrim at Kailash,
1990. © Katia Buffetrille

17. Bönpo pilgrims at Kailash,
1990 © Katia Buffetrille

Amnye Machen, on the other hand, is a mountain on which the two concepts are still superimposed: "territorial god," *yüllha*, and "Buddhist holy place" mountain (*neri*). The process of Buddhicisation is still going on, as I witnessed during the four pilgrimages I made in 1990, 1992, 2002 and 2018. Until recently, pilgrimage guides dedicated to this mountain were very scarce. Today, new ones are published fairly regularly. They depict Amnye Machen as a *bodhisattva* — an altruistic being who develops the aspiration to enlightenment, *bodhicitta*, working for the well-being of others — and sometimes even as a Buddha, while the surrounding landscape is presented in a manner resembling the Demchog *mandala*.

The mountain is even a *mandala* in itself. One guide identifies Amnye Machen with a *mandala* populated by divine assemblies gathered around the "glorious Demchog," crisscrossed by "innumerable goddesses of offerings" carrying "objects of offerings in infinite number" and doing the "circumambulation" of the *mandala*. Unlike Kailash, there are numerous iconographic representations of the god Amnye Machen. These representations are common in the entrance hall of Amdo monasteries.

There is a particularly propitious year for the pilgrimage (the horse-year), but not a specific date. Pilgrims come as the weather and their work permit. Moreover, in the

18. Amnye Machen mountain,
1992 © Katia Buffetrille

1990s, pilgrims were essentially nomads from the surrounding regions, for whom this mountain is the most important "territorial god" of the area. Their behaviour showed that they came to a non-Buddhist mountain deity: many of them were on horseback while every Buddhist knows that such a pilgrimage brings few merits (*sönam*); others carried rifles or swords. They performed rituals not prescribed by the pilgrimage guides: they lifted very heavy stones or weighed their sins by hanging a rock ledge, actions that belong to a religious background of non-Buddhist beliefs. And it was to Amnye Machen, their territorial god, that they addressed their requests, since they knew he was the one able to fulfil their desires for earthly boons.

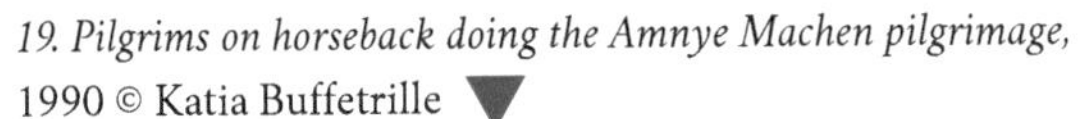

19. Pilgrims on horseback doing the Amnye Machen pilgrimage,
1990 © Katia Buffetrille ▼

▲ *20. Pilgrim carrying a gun,*
1990 © Katia Buffetrille

Little by little, roads are being built around every sacred mountain. While a pilgrim on foot follows the 'traces' that delineates the sacred space, the new roads have little regard for them and one wonders if the process of modernisation affecting the sacred mountains and the surrounding landscape will prove an obstacle to the growing Buddhicisation. Thus, at Amnye Machen, the recent construction of a road has changed both the pilgrimage experience and the landscape to a significant degree.

The modern road deviates from the old trail, which followed the riverbed and required the crossing of many fords. As a result, the new road is condemning some sacred sites to oblivion, while creating new ones. Nowadays, pilgrims who come by car stop only at important sites, and only if these sites are on the side of the road. At the same time, their offerings (prayer flags *-lungta-*, fragrant smoke offerings-*sang*) are much more bigger, as if to compensate for the absence of physical effort with an increase in the quantity of offerings.

On the other hand, the modern road allows people with limited spare time, as well as the very old, to make their own pilgrimages. One also comes across pilgrims who come from distant places and who take advantage of modern amenities to make pilgrimages they would not have undertaken otherwise.

21. The pilgrimage road follows at some points the highwaygoing from the Golok Tibetan Autonomous Prefecture to Chengdu (820 km)

22. Offerings at Tamchog Gongkha Pass,
2018 © Katia Buffetrille

But the road is not the only problem threatening many sacred mountains, including Amnye Machen. There is also the exploitation of mineral resources. Tibetans regularly protest to demand respect for the sacred spaces and the end of the destruction and pollution caused by exploitation. A Tibetan poet expresses his fears and pain in the following poem:[2]

2 http://highpeakspureearth.com/2012/poem-to-amnye-machen/ (Access 21 February 2019).

"To Amnye Machen"

Author: The Plateau is my Home

Even though I have never seen you,
Even though I have never been at your side,
I know your stalwart figure
Standing firmly in the boundless space
between heaven and earth.

On your venerable forehead that has
passed through thousands of years
Are the clean snowflakes shin-
ing in the sun of the Plateau.
Under your vast, peaceful and smooth feet
Resound songs of praises to you
by the plateau herders.
You are one of the nine sacred mountains of Tibet.
Your fame is firmly established throughout the world.
You are the Dharma defender of Amdo.
Your good name is widely known.

However, today, the wheels of greed
Are running over the grassland, enter-
ing directly under your feet.
They bring bombs, trucks, and excavators,
And other bizarre tools that are used by demons
To excavate the hidden gems from your body

The people who have been guard-
ing you for millions of years
Are unable to guard you anymore
They can only endure in silence
Their only choice is to wait helplessly.
One day they will be forced to move out,
Saying goodbye tearfully to your beau-
tiful and warm embrace.
Where will they go?
They will be placed on the edge of the barren desert.

Henceforth, on our sacred Amnye Machen,
The white flocks of sheep will never be seen again.
The song of the herders will never be heard again.
Those filthy greedy people will
soon mercilessly stifle you.

nam dag yum gyi dkyil 'khor ▶
Mandala of the Totally Pure Mother
Acrylic and mineral color on canvas
86 x 86 cm
2013

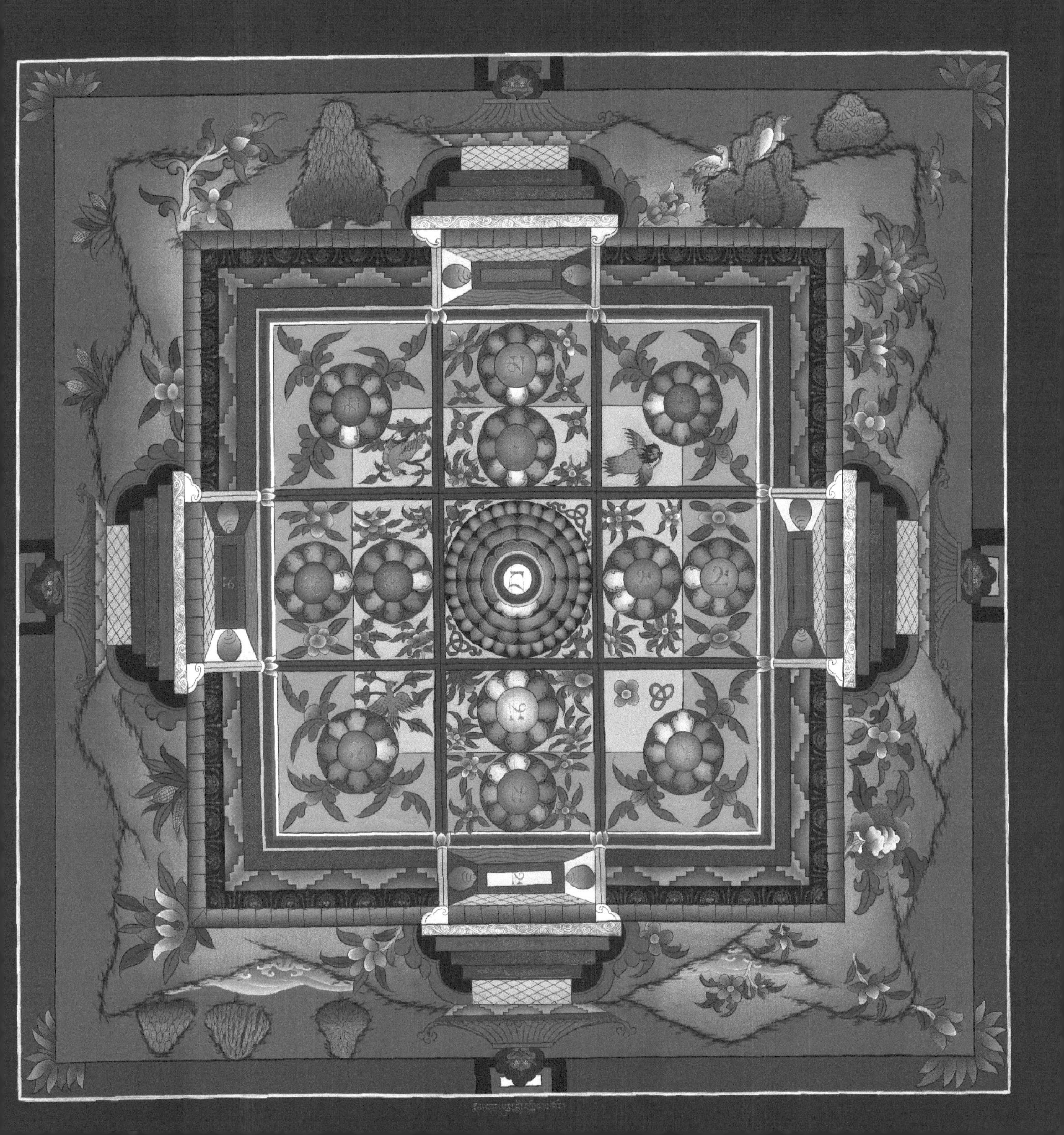

KUBUM AND SE'U GANG: TWO TEMPLES FORMERLY NAMED GYUNG DRUNG BON IN BHUTAN

Françoise Pommaret

Françoise Pommaret

Research Director Centre de recherche sur les civilisations de l'Asie orientale,
CNRS and Assistant Professor at the College of Language and Culture Studies – ILCS – Royal University of Bhutan

Kubum (*sKu 'bum*) and Se'u gang (*rTsi ba sgang*) are two complementary temples which belonged to the gYung Drung Bon tradition in Bhutan and were linked to the prominent tertön Dorje Lingpa (*rDo rje gling pa* – 1346-1405). Dorje Lingpa was an eclectic religious figure, who was Bon (under the name *Bon zhig gling pa or gYung drung gling pa*) as well as Buddhist. Around 1370-71, he stayed in the Shar region (nowadays the district of Wangdu Phodrang), in the west of Bhutan, before heading towards Bumthang in Central Bhutan.

In the autumn of 1370, he taught at the temple of Kubum, which was founded by Dru Tshanden Dulwa Gyaltshen (*Bru mTshan Idan 'Dul ba rgyal mtshan* – 1239-1293) in

the upper valley of Phobjikha (*Pho sbis kha*). This Bonpo lama who originated in Central Tibet also founded Se'u gang in a lower valley of the Shar region, where Ddorje Lingpa stayed as well; the two temples still show traces of propitiation to the Bon deity Sipey Gyalmo (*Srid pa'i rgyal mo*).

The exact circumstances of the foundation of these two temples by Tshanden Dulwa Gyaltshen during the 13th century AD are still unknown, as is the reason why he chose this region.

These two temples are located in the valleys that nomads used as seasonal residences, as often happened in Bhutan. In summer, the villagers used to migrate close to Kubum, in the upper valley of Phobjika, at an altitude of 3,000 metres; in winter, the same villagers migrated back to an altitude of 1,800 metres, to the semi-tropical region of Se'ugang and the village of Gelekha, where they owned fields. Sipey Gyalmo, the protective deity, travelled with them and the local name of Se'ugang refers to the meal the deity reputedly had at this place.

Since the end of 1990s, the temples have been restored and are now under the control of the Drukpa Kagyu and Nyingma schools. Nevertheless, daily propitiation to the deity Sipey Gyalmo still continues. This deity is also venerated by villagers for different reasons, such as victory in archery tournaments, safe travelling and naming babies. Kunley, who was the guardian of the temple in 2007, used to call her *Am*, "Mother," as in the Bonpo tradition where she is called "*My* Mother."

For more information see: Karmay, S. (2002). Dorje Lingpa and his rediscovery of the 'Gold Needle' in Bhutan. *Journal of Bhutan Studies, 2* (2), 1-34.

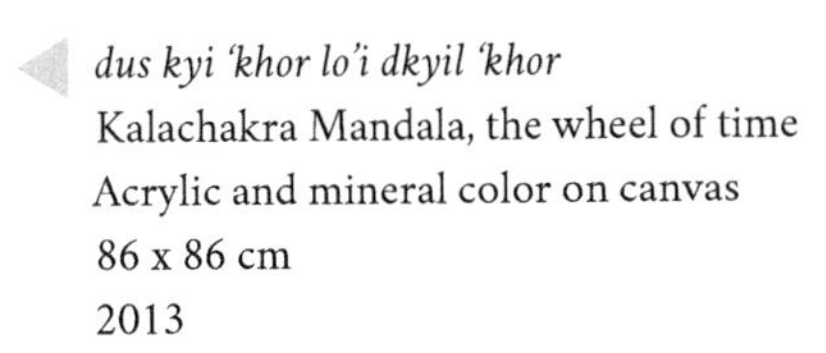

dus kyi 'khor lo'i dkyil 'khor
Kalachakra Mandala, the wheel of time
Acrylic and mineral color on canvas
86 x 86 cm
2013

THE POTENTIAL BENEFIT OF TRADITIONAL HIMALAYAN MIND-BODY PRACTICES IN MODERN OCCIDENTAL SOCIETY

Alejandro Chaoul

Introduction

Alejandro Chaoul, PhD

The Himalayan traditions are rich in mind-body practices, utilizing them for spiritual development, as a tool towards enlightenment, and, secondarily, for physical and emotional well-being. This article will focus on the manner in which some of the Tibetan Bön Yoga of Channels-breath (*rTsa rLung*)[3] and Magical movements (*'Phrul 'Khor*) have been practiced among Tibetan and Himalayan communities, as well as some more recent applications within contemporary western clinical settings which were developed as these practices migrated outside of Tibet and the Indian subcontinent.

Channel-breaths and Magical movements are distinctive Tibetan mind-body practices in which breath and concentration of the

3 Borrowing from David Germano's translation "channel-winds practices" (Germano 1994), I will use the term "channel breaths" practices. I feel this translates the Tibetan phrase accurately and brings a better sense of the subject matter: a specific practice that utilises the channels and different aspects of breath.

mind are integrated with particular body movements. They have been part of spiritual training among Tibetan yogis since at least the tenth century ce. The globalization of the twentieth century has not only allowed many of the Asian mind-body practices to take root in the West, but some practitioners have also adopted what anthropologist Joseph Alter calls the "medicalisation" of modern yoga (Alter, 2005). In other words, there's an emphasis on the healing properties of yoga, sometimes even further than the original texts would go. These concepts, I believe, stem from the intimate relationship that these yogic practices have with their medical counterparts (*haṭha yoga with ayurveda, rtsa rlung 'phrul 'khor with gSo ba rig pa* or Tibetan medicine) and from their arrival in the West at this time to become part of the emerging field of integrative medicine.

Mind-body practices such as meditation and yoga have become extremely popular in Europe and the U.S. in the last couple of decades as a way to reduce stress and enhance spiritual growth. This is particularly true for some categories of patients.[4] For example, many people who suffer from cancer believe that stress plays a role in the aetiology and progression of their condition. Although there is no evidence that stress causes cancer, research shows that stress does have an active role in cancer progression. (Lutgendrof, Sood, et al., 2010)

Tibetan medical texts, from both the Bönpo *Medical Collection ('Bum bzhi)* and the Buddhist *Four Tantras (rGyud bzhi)*,[5] explain the "science of healing" (*gSo ba rig pa*) or Tibetan Medicine, in terms of balance of one's internal constitution, defined by the three nyes pa (sometimes translated in English as

4 Jon Kabat-Zinn's Mindfulness Based Stress Reduction (MBSR) programme at the University of Massachussetts Medical School pioneered this area of study. Through clinical applications and research, it opened a way toward acceptance of meditative programmes in the field of medicine. It is still a small, yet significant, opening in the Western medical system at large.

5 Bön is the native religious tradition of Tibet, that claims its origins in Buddha Tonpa Shenrab 18,000 years ago. The tradition's holy texts, including the *'Bum bzhi*, claim its origins from Tönpa Shenrab and, therefore, it considers itself to be older than the *rGyud bzhi*. However, there are some debates regarding its origins and the relation between Bön and the tradition that we call now Buddhism.

"humours"),[6] and the five cosmo-physical elements (*'byung*). Health in this context is not solely a concern with the body's illness or disease, but, most importantly, the harmony of body, energy and mind.

Among the three humours, *rlung* – the "wind" humour – is described as having five distinctive kinds. Interestingly, the Bönpo *Mother Tantra (Ma rgyud)* describes a set of five channel-breaths *(rtsa rlung)* yogic movements, where each movement is explained in terms of those same five breaths/winds *(rlung)* as in the Tibetan medical system (also equivalent to those in the Indian medical system of Ayurveda). These channel-breaths are linked to the five cosmo-physical elements (Samlek, 1971).

Over fifteen years ago, in 2000, after I spent a year facilitating a Tibetan meditation class at The Place of Wellness (now the Integrative Medicine Center), at The University of Texas M.D. Anderson Cancer Center (M.D. Anderson), Dr. Lorenzo Cohen, a behavioural researcher there and now director of their Integrative Medicine Program, asked me to propose a research intervention based on the Tibetan mind-body practices that could be applied to people with cancer. After asking for the approval and support of my Tibetan teachers, Yongdzin Tenzin Namdak and Tenzin Wangyal Rinpoche, I joined a research team, led by Dr. Cohen, with the aim of investigating the possible effects of a Tibetan mind-body intervention for people with cancer.

In this setting, "mind-body" refers to the experience of our existence as a whole, instead of having our mind experience isolated from that of our body. The Tibetan traditions also explain what I like to call the "missing link" between "mind" and "body." That link is "energy" (*rtsal*), which is mostly expressed as speech and breath. Intervention, in the western clinical research setting, refers to a particular programme design, in this case Tibetan yoga, with a particular population, in this case cancer patients, where this programme may help improve an aspect of health in this population.

In this article, I will present some of the research into the use of Tibetan yogic practices as interventions for people with cancer,

6 See Barbara Gerke's discussion of the appropriation of the word "humour" for *nyes pa* (Gerke, 2011), especially pp. 128-30.

including some of the challenges, results and conclusions. These studies were conducted at M.D. Anderson's Integrative Medicine Program, where the aim, following Engel's seminal paper in *Science* in 1977, is to provide healing focused not just on the physical (i.e., bio) but also on the psycho-social-spiritual aspects of the person, something that seems to be forgotten in conventional allopathic medicine (Engel, 1977, where he speaks of the need for a bio-psycho-social-spiritual model that would supplement the current biomedical model).

Tibetan Yoga Research

Since 2000, the research teams of M.D. Anderson and the Ligmincha Institute (an international centre for Bön study and practice founded by Tenzin Wangyal Rinpoche, with its main retreat centre in Shipman, Virginia, and over 30 centres all over the world, including one in Houston, Texas) have engaged in research, while also teaching groups and individuals how to support people touched by cancer in their illness experience (see Arthur Kleinman, *Illness Narratives*, where he describes the difference of disease – in this case, cancer – vs. the whole illness experience that the patient and the family are going through).

As I mention elsewhere (Chaoul, 2007a, 2007b and 2011), we began with two pilot studies involving randomized controlled trials (RCT), with one for people suffering from lymphoma and the other for women with breast cancer. We used a Tibetan Yoga (TY) intervention that included not only the Channels-breath practices from the Bön *Mother Tantra* but also the Magical movements practices from the *Oral Transmission of Zhang Zhung (Zhang zhung snyan rgyud).* These pilot studies were among the few RCT studies of yoga in a cancer patient population at the time, as well as the first scientific studies of Tibetan yoga in any patient population. The results suggested that these ancient Tibetan Bön yogic practices may be beneficial adjuncts to conventional medicine and may have a significant contribution to the well-being and quality of life of people suffering from cancer (Cohen, et al., 2004, Chaoul, 2007a, 2007b and 2011, and Chandwani, et al., 2008, Leal, et al., 2015).

With that precedent and findings (see Cohen, et al., 2004), the U.S. National Institutes of Health (NIH) awarded in 2006 a large National Cancer Institute grant to the teams to support a five-year randomized trial to examine a TY programme for women undergoing chemotherapy for breast cancer. Based on the feedback of previous participants and instructors, the intervention was adjusted to focus more exclusively on the Channels-breath Tibetan yogic practices from the Bön *Mother Tantra*. This work has not only put Western scientific ideas on medical research in dialogue with Tibetan *dharmic* practice, but it has also prompted both sides to take steps toward finding a sound methodology and, more importantly, brought some benefit to cancer patients and their families.

The intervention, chosen in consultation with Tenzin Wangyal Rinpoche, consisted of three main components: 1) breathing exercises; 2) meditative concentration; 3) Channels-breath sitting yogic postures. These components have been used in the Bön tradition for centuries and were chosen as an intervention specific for cancer patients undergoing chemotherapy or having completed treatment in the last twelve months, with the intention of facilitating their recovery and offsetting the side effects of their treatments. Participants were taught this programme as a progressive didactic

and experiential set of classes with the aim of helping the patient incorporate these techniques into their everyday lives. From the Tibetan tradition perspective, these practices clear away obstacles (gegs sel)[7] and enhance one's meditative state of mind (*bog don*) in order to incorporate the elevated meditative state of mind into everyday behaviour (*spyod pa*). The breathing exercises help participants regulate their breath, calm their minds and remove physical, emotional and mental obstacles. The meditative concentration techniques help harness the calmness of mind towards self-observation and use the breathing exercises to remove obstacles.

Commenting on these yogic practices, the great 19th-20th century Tibetan Bönpo scholar and meditator, Shardza Tashi Gyaltsen, instructs the practitioner that in order to advance on the path of Channels-breath practices, one must first train in the concentration of the mind and avoid falling after deluded thoughts (Shardza, 1974b: 28). Thus, not only the breathing is emphasized but the concentration of the mind with it. In fact, in the patient's manual this is named after the *Mother Tantra's* metaphor of the "rider and the horse," where the horse refers to the breath and the rider to the mind guiding it. Therefore, the participants begin their training with this meditative technique to help them calm and focus their mind, utilizing their breath to train their focus and concentration.

The Channels-breath movements work by applying those meditative concentration techniques and breathing exercises to different areas of the physical body. Once the participants learn and practice these movements, they are introduced to the subtle body as an inner structure, with its energetic centres or *chakras*. This deeper engagement with the practice helps participants to relax and feel invigorated, as well as to cleanse different areas of their bodies (and subtle bodies) by integrating the movements with the meditative and breathing techniques. All classes were taught by instructors authorized by the Ligmincha Institute. The classes were one-and-a-half hour sessions, with four classes held once a week (or every three weeks for those undergoing chemotherapy), followed by three booster sessions once a month.[8] This gave participants the opportunity to learn the techniques and practice them with the instructor, so that they could continue to practice on their own. At the end of each class, the participants received printed materials and DVDs to take home to help them in their home practice. The

7 Although many times written as *bgegs*, this type of "obstacle" or "hindrance" is spelled *gegs* in Shardza 1974a, and in Chandra and Namdak 1968 as *gags*. Thus far I have not been able to find if there are any significant differences in meanings among them.

8 We changed the intervention to four sessions of half an hour instead of seven sessions of one hour, because many of the women had chemotherapy sessions every three weeks, which would have pushed our course to 21 weeks. The stretching or active control group followed the same schedule.

practices were described in an accessible manner, while the manual included illustrative photographs.[9] Patients were also asked to log in their practice times on special pages of their manuals. At the end of the course, the participants were given DVDs and CDs containing guided practices of all the techniques. The patients turned their practice logs over to the research team. Participants were advised to practice daily at home, in addition to the classes at the clinic, and to continue their exercises after the course was over.

The study measured the possible stress relief, improvement of Quality of Life (QOL) and immune system level (through blood analysis), as well as the reduction of anxiety and sleep disturbances that the TY intervention can provide to women undergoing chemotherapy for breast cancer, in comparison to the two control groups: those doing a series of stretching exercises[10] and those receiving what is called the "standard of care," which in this case does not include any particular intervention. The two control groups were wait list control groups, following the same measures and assessment times. Thus, the participants making up the two control groups have the opportunity to receive the TY programme after the twelve-month follow-up assessment –hence the name "wait list." In addition, the study measured outcomes in terms of psychosocial models of benefit finding and spirituality.

In clinical research, we should provide the kind of intervention that we believe is the most suitable and effective for our patients, as we draw from the wisdom of these ancient traditions. In medical research institutions such as M.D. Anderson, and in particular within the area of complementary and integrative medicine (CIM), these Tibetan Yoga studies may provide the right context to turn this beginning into an opportunity to bridge both sides and create an easier way for patients to incorporate conceptually and experientially the use mind-body practices.

The breast cancer patients included in the TY study learned the nine breathings of purification (*dgu rlung sang*), which is a common foundational set of breathing exercises among Bönpo practitioners, both lay and monastic, and similar to the nine-breathings sets of other Tibetan Buddhist traditions. Once they learned the mechanics of this set of breathings, the participants were taught the inner structure and physiology of the subtle body. Tibetan texts explain that the vital breath currents cannot flow in the proper way, together with the mind, through the channels when the mind is distracted by one of the afflictions, such as anger (*zhe sdang*),

9 See photographs of some of the movements that were part of the intervention. Photos by Andreas Zihler, to whom I want to express my gratitude.

10 The stretching movements came from breast cancer exercise manuals (Davis, 2002; Halverstadt and Leonard, 2000) and were chosen to match, in the best possible way, the physical component of the channel-breaths movements.

attachment (*'dod chags*) and unawareness or "foggy mind" (*gti mugs*). Thus, with the help of the nine breathings of purifications, patients can get help in relieving some of their discomfort.

Tenzin Wangyal Rinpoche emphasizes that it is important that the discomfort in question be "fresh, personal and recent" (Wangyal, 2008).[11] In other words, working on something that patients think they might feel or on things they try to remember from their childhoods does not have the same impact. Instead, working on something they experience as a personal obstacle at that very moment will have a greater impact. Cancer patients tend to focus on physical pain and anecdotally report how, after the exercises, the pain diminishes and even disappears. The patients in the Tibetan Yoga group had a greater sense of acceptance and found a greater sense of meaning in their illness (Leal, et al., 2014).

Others have mentioned how their anxiety is reduced after just one session. In other words, some of their obstacles are reduced or dissolved. Tenzin Wangyal Rinpoche emphasizes the importance of the "transformation" that occurs when practicing these powerful methods. Therefore, utilizing these ancient practices in this way can be seen as constituting a way of breaking open the space of biomedicine to include these benefits in its repertoire. Or, simply expressed, perhaps we can think about such dialogues as possible bridges to communicate the wisdom of these ancient practices to scientists, patients and practitioners.

11 Tenzin Wangyal Rinpoche, personal conversation with the instructors of the TY programme for people with cancer, Houston, February 2008.

The Three Channels

The channels (*rtsa*) are the architectural support of the subtle body and act as pathways through which fluids and energies travel. Some, like the veins and arteries, are the pathways for blood to circulate around our body. Subtler channels are the roads through which vital breath (*rlung*) currents travel, nurturing the subtler dimensions of the body.

Indian and Tibetan tantric literature offers detailed descriptions of the principal three channels of the subtle body,[12] and the *Mother Tantra* follows the same path in defining those three channels. The description offered to patients is simple. Rather than calling them by their Sanskrit or Tibetan names, we use the terms Central, Right and Left channels, supported by the visualization of their respective blue, white, and red colours. The importance of the central channel and of bringing the mind's attention and breath into the central channel is also discussed with patients in simple terms. In fact, the central channel is introduced first, while the side channels are "added" in subsequent sessions. Patients are encouraged first to imagine, then visualize and then feel those channels as made of light and being flexible, so that when vital breath travels through them one can feel them inflate like balloons.[13]

12 The general agreement in Hindu and Buddhist subtle body descriptions is that there are three channels of utmost importance: a "central channel" (dbu ma, suṣumnā), or "all-encompassing" channel (kun 'dar ma, avadhūtī) sometimes known as the "Royal Road" (Avalon, 1958), flanked on the right by the white-coloured "solitary" channel (rkyang ma, piṅgalā), and flanked on the left by the red-coloured "flavour" (ro ma, iḍā).

13 H.H. Lungtok Tenpa'i Nyima mentioned how Tibetans would traditionally use the metaphor of intestines (*rgyu ma*) as channels, but felt that the balloon metaphor may seem more appropriate for a western audience (Menri monastery, oral communication, 2002).

The Five Energetic Centres

Along this supporting structure of channels lie the energetic centres or *chakras*. Their numbers and locations vary according to the tradition describing them and even according to the specific practice in which they are involved, but the most important ones are generally those located along the central channel. The *Mother Tantra* mentions five chakras engaged by the Channels-breath (*rtsa rlung*) practice: Crown, Throat, Heart, Navel, and Secret. Patients are introduced to them not only conceptually, but also experientially by bringing the breath supported with the mind's attention to each energetic centre, and then applying the prescribed channels-breath movement.

sku gsum don grub mkha' 'gying dkar po'i dkyil 'khor
Mandala of the White Sky Dancing (deity),
the realization of the State of Three Kayas (three nlightened bodies)
Acrylic and mineral color on canvas
67 x 67 cm
2013

The Five Vital Breaths

The Channels-breath movements described in the *Mother Tantra* correlate with five kinds of vital breath currents (*rlung*). Shardza, basing his description on the *Mother Tantra*, describes the five vital breath currents as follows (Shardza, 1974b: 28):[14]

- UPWARD MOVING (GYEN DU RGYU) VITAL BREATH AT THE CENTRE OF THE THROAT,
- LIFE UPHOLDING OR LIFE FORCE (SROG 'DZIN PA) VITAL BREATH AT THE CENTRE OF THE HEART,
- FIRE AND EQUANIMITY (MNYAM PA) VITAL BREATHS AT THE CENTRE OF THE NAVEL,
- DOWNWARD (THUR DU) CLEARING (SEL BA) VITAL BREATH AT THE SECRET CENTRE,
- PERVASIVE (KHYAB) VITAL BREATH IN ALL THE CHANNEL PETALS – OR CONNECTIONS WITH ALL SMALLER CHANNELS.

Shardza writes that, in channels-breath practices, one brings the air with one-pointed concentration (*sems gtad*) to each energetic centre (Shardza, 1974). By engaging in these yogic practices, practitioners and patients can produce that shift or transformation. Allowing the air to move along and around (*gyi gyi kor kor*) each of the centres, as one performs the Channels-breath practices, one helps the clearing of those areas and the mind to focus better and rest more comfortably. From the practitioner's perspective, these yogic practices provide the methods to transform from the state of an ordinary sentient being into that of an enlightened being, a Buddha (*rsangs rgyas*). For patients, the goal is to have these methods help them relieve discomforts (pain, anxiety, emotional distress, intrusive thoughts, etc.), improve their quality of life and sleep better. Patients notice that, when such changes occur, they also feel more connected to themselves and others, which is also encouraged in the instructions by connecting to one's inner

14 Shardza. (1974b: 28). Also *Mother Tantra*, pp. 603ff.

home and sharing the benefits with others.[15] Patients also comment that they feel empowered by these practices and the experience of sharing the benefits with others. Although we are still preparing to publish these results, what is noticeable is that participants need to practice at least twice a week or more to obtain the benefits we observed in the pilot studies. This is an important issue for researchers and practitioners. In other words, mind-body practices need to be included in one's lifestyle in the same way that physical exercise is seen as an important part of a healthy lifestyle. Some more comprehensive lifestyle studies, such as those by Dean Ornish[16] and an ongoing M.D. Anderson protocol based on David Servan-Schreiber's book Anticancer: A new way of Life, (Servan-Schreiber, 2007)[17] emphasize what is also recommended clinically at the Integrative Medicine Center: optimal health requires a healthy diet, enough exercise, a mind-body practice and good social support.

To also address the issue of social support, with the addition of a new researcher, social psychologist Kathrin Milbury, in our latest Tibetan Yoga study we decided to focus not only on the patient, but also on the caregiver. Calling it TYC (Tibetan Yoga for Couples), this single-arm pilot study was designed for people suffering from lung cancer and their caregivers living in the same home, usually their spouse or partner. This intervention included the nine breathings of purification, as well as two of the five Channels-breath movements, particularly the ones that addressed the area of the chest related to life force vital breath, and the pervasive breath movement that includes a self-massage of the whole body. For patients in the TYC group, significant

15 There is more evidence of enhanced well-being thanks to social support, which can also be related to the concept of sangha, or spiritual community.

16 For over 35 years, Dean Ornish, M.D., and his colleagues have conducted a series of research studies showing that changes in diet and lifestyle can make a powerful difference in our health and well-being, including improvements in cardiovascular disease and cancer (see for example, "Intensive Lifestyle Changes for Reversal of Coronary Heart Disease" Ornish, D. et al., *JAMA*, December 16, 1998—Vol 280, No. 23, and "Changes in prostate gene expression in men undergoing an intensive nutrition and lifestyle intervention", Ornish D. et al. *PNAS* June 17, 2008 vol. 105 no. 24 8369–8374).

17 Servan-Schreiber, David, M.D. PhD, *Anticancer: A New Way of Life*, Paris: Robert Laffont, 2007, English translation, UK: Penguin Books, 2008

improvements were primarily revealed in the areas of spiritual well-being and benefit finding, which may be of great value to patients considering their general poor prognosis. A moderate impact was detected in depressive symptoms and sleep disturbances, with corresponding reductions in clinical levels. Caregivers in the TYC group reported significantly less fatigue and anxiety compared to the baseline ratings (large impact) and marginally significantly less sleep disturbances as seen in the mean difference scores (moderate impact), as well as reductions in clinical levels. A moderate impact was found for caregivers regarding benefit finding (Milbury, Chaoul, et al., 2014).

Moving Forward to More Healing Opportunities

The Tibetan Yogic studies mentioned above are among those which highlight the possible efficacy of meditative and yogic techniques that exist in some centuries-old Asian traditions and reinforce the idea that applying them in Western medical settings can bring results. In the model used in this study, the movements can function as a tool that makes the integration with the contemplative aspect easier than a meditation session with no movement. Therefore, patients can use the movements to learn to guide their minds and vital breath currents through the channels into different areas, opening themselves up to the possibility of healing or harmonizing body, energy and mind, also known as the body-energy-mind system. This is a goal shared by yogic practices, and it is also a model of good health that is in line with the concept of health or well-being in Tibetan medicine (Dhonden, 1986). Tibetan texts do not explicitly mention among benefits such concepts as stress reduction, the elimination of intrusive thoughts, or improvement of sleep. However, as the head teacher of Menri monastery in India, Lopon Thinley Nyima, states, these and other related outcomes may be included as secondary benefits related to the removal of obscurations (Thinley, 2005, lecture).[18] In other words, as the channels open up, the breath travelling through them, guided by one's mind's attention, brings experiences of mind-energy-body healing.

Many Tibetan doctors have also expressed support for and interest in our studies over the years (Chaoul, 2011). Dr Yangbum Gyal stated that,

> *"Overall, working with the five **lung** with **tsalung** revitalises the body and mind by balancing and promoting the free flow of prana or **lung**-energy. Regular **tsalung***

18 Ponlob Thinley Nyima, 'Mind-body practices of the ancient Tibetan Bön tradition', talk at Rice University, Houston, TX, April 2005.

exercises relieve muscular tension and nervous stress, improve breathing and digestion, benefit the cardiovascular system and lead to deep relaxation and well-being." (Gyal, 2007, personal communication).

This is also in agreement with the emerging fields of CIM and behavioural science, which include yogic practices as part of their Mind and Body category.[19] These fields use both objective and subjective measurements, such as the ones mentioned in our studies.

Interestingly, although the concept of measurement may seem counterintuitive to contemplative practices, it is found in Tibetan yogic texts and oral instructions. However, the measurements are not done by drawing out blood or saliva for analysis or by filling out charts to determine stress levels, mood or anxiety, or if patients sleep well. The texts speak not only of removing obstacles, as mentioned earlier, but also of measuring the heat that related practices (i.e. *gtum mo* or "inner heat") may create by the number of breaths needed to dry an almost frozen towel placed on the practitioner's bare back, or the time needed to wet a dry towel with their perspiration, or methods of counting how long one can hold one's breath during a particular exercise. Clearly such measurements are not the same as those utilized in Western biomedical sciences or CIM, but these examples can provide a glimpse into the idea that qualitative and quantitative measuring is not totally absent from Tibetan yogic traditions. Furthermore, many contemporary Tibetan lamas have shown interest and support for this kind of scientific research into the contemplative practices. In our own research, the constant support of Tenzin Wangyal Rinpoche has been vital to the integrity of our studies.

In addition to the Tibetan Yoga studies, we have also done research on the Tibetan

19 The National Center for Complementary and Integrative Medicine (NCCAM) recently changed its name to the National Center Complementary Integrative Health (NCCIH), and the former category of mind-body practices has been absorbed into the larger category of mind and body practices that includes massage, acupuncture, chiropractic, etc. Research in mind-body practices has increased dramatically in the last decade. Many studies have focused on how meditation may be helpful for a variety of conditions, such as high blood pressure, certain psychological disorders, and pain. A number of studies have also helped researchers learn how meditation might work and how it affects the brain (see https://nccih.nih.gov/health/mindbody, accessed 6/24/2016). Mind-body practices show promise in relieving the effects of cancer and cancer treatment.

Sound Meditation (TSM) for women suffering from breast cancer who felt cognitive impairment after chemotherapy (sometimes called chemobrain). These patients followed a simpler version of Tenzin Wangyal Rinpoche's Tibetan Sound Healing (Wangyal, 2006) and his personal advice. We published the findings of our first pilot study (Milbury, Chaoul, et al., 2013) and we are in the middle of a study that involves not only M.D. Anderson in Houston, but also the Einstein Hospital in Sao Paulo, Brazil. The TSM research will be included in a future article.

As these studies continue, all of us who participate in them are constantly being reshaped, which in turn reshapes the fields in which we work, such as integrative medicine. I hope that these Tibetan Yoga research studies contribute in a small way to the exploration of a new kind of medicine, one that includes science and spirituality, and highlights the importance of mind-body practices as part of a healthy lifestyle, not only for the ultimate truth of healing (i.e., enlightenment), but also for the conventional truth of bio-psycho-social as optimal health.

byams ldan rgyal ba'i dkyil 'khor
Mandala of the Loving Victor
Acrylic and mineral color on canvas
86 x 86 cm
2013

References

Alter, J.S. (2005). Modern Medical Yoga. Struggling with a History of Magic, Alchemy and Sex. *Asian Medicine*, 1(1), 119–46.

Avalon, A. (Sir John Woodroffe) (1958). *The Serpent Power*. Madras, India: Ganesh & Co.

Benson, H., et al., (1982). Body temperature changes during the practice of gTum-mo yoga. *Nature*, 295, 234-236.

Chandra, L., & Namdak, T. (Eds.) (1968). The Great Perfection Oral Transmission of Zhang Zhung (*Rdzogs pa chen po Zhang zhung snyan rgyud*): History and Doctrines of Bonpo Nispanna Yoga. New Delhi, India: *International Academy of Indian Culture*.

Chandwani, K.D., Chaoul, M.A., & Cohen, L. (2008). Mind-Body Research in Cancer. in L. Cohen and M. Markman (Eds.), *Integrative Oncology: Incorporating Complementary Medicine into Conventional Cancer Care* (pp.139-61). Totowa, New Jersey: Humana Press.

Chaoul, M.A. (2007a). Magical Movements (*'phrul 'khor*) in the Bon Tradition and Possible Applications as a CIM (Complementary and Integrative Medicine) Therap. In M. Schrempf (Ed.), *Soundings in Tibetan Medicine: Anthropological and Historical Perspectives* (pp. 285-304). Proceedings of the International Association of Tibetan Studies (PIATS), 2003, Leiden, The Netherlands: Brill.

__________. (2007b). Magical Movements (*'phrul 'khor*): Ancient Tibetan Yogic Practices from the Bon Religion and their Migration to Contemporary Medical Settings. *Asian Medicine*, 3(1), 130-155.

__________. (2011). Re-integrating the Dharmic Perspective in Bio-Behavioural Research of a "Tibetan Yoga" (*tsalung trülkhor*) Intervention for People with Cancer. In V. Adams, M. Schrempf and S. Craig (Eds.), *Medicine between Science and Religion* (pp. 297-318). Oxford, UK: Berghahn.

Cohen, L., et al. (2004). Psychological Adjustment and Sleep Quality in a Randomized Trial of the Effects of a Tibetan Yoga Intervention in Patients with Lymphoma. *Cancer: Interdisciplinary Journal of the American Cancer Society, 100*(10), 2253–60.

Davis, S.L. (2002). *Thriving After Breast Cancer: Essential Exercises for Body and Mind.* New York: Broadway Books.

Dhonden, Y. (2000). *Healing from the Source.* Ithaca, New York: Snow Lion Publications.

Engel, G.L. (1977). The Need for a New Medical Model: A Challenge for Biomedicine. *Science, New Series,* 196(4286), 129-136.

Germano, D. (1994). *Mini-Encyclopedia of Great Perfection Terminology.* (unpublished manuscript), Charlottesville: University of Virginia.

Gerke, B. (2011). Correlating Biomedical and Tibetan Terms in Amchi Medical Practice. In V. Adams, M. Schrempf and S. Craig (Eds.), *Medicine Between Science and Religion: Explorations on Tibetan Grounds* (pp.127-152). New York and Oxford, UK: Berghahn Books.

Halverstadt, A. & Leonard, A. (2000). *Essential Exercises for Breast Cancer Survivors.* Boston, Massachusetts: The Harvard Common Press.

Kleinman, A. (1988). *The Illness Narratives: Suffering, Healing and the Human Condition,* New York: Basic Books.

Leal I., Engebretson J., Cohen L., Rodriguez A., Wangyal T., Lopez G., Chaoul A. (2014). Experiences of paradox: a qualitative analysis of living with cancer using a framework approach. *Psychooncology 24*(2).138-46.

Lutgendorf S.K., Sood A.K., Antoni M.H. (2010). Host factors and cancer progression: biobehavioral signaling pathways and interventions. J *Clin Oncol, 28*(26), 4094–9.

Milbury K., Chaoul A., Engle R., Liao Z., Yang C., Carmack C., Shannon V., Spelman A., Wangyal T., Cohen L. (2015). Couple-Based Tibetan Yoga Program for Lung Cancer Patients and their Caregivers. *Psychooncology 24*(1),117-20.

Milbury, K., et al. (2013). Tibetan sound meditation for cognitive dysfunction: results of a randomized controlled pilot trial. Psychooncology. DOI: 10.1002/pon.3296

Ornish, D., et al. (1998). Intensive Lifestyle Changes for Reversal of Coronary Heart Disease. Journal of the American Medical Association (JAMA), 280(23). DOI: 10.1001/jama.280.23.2001

__________. (2008). Changes in prostate gene expression in men undergoing an intensive nutrition and lifestyle intervention. *Proceedings of the National Academy of Sciences (PNAS), 105*(24), 8369–8374.

Samlek, M. (Rgyal gshen Mi lus bsam legs), (1985). *Ma rgyud thugs rje nyi ma'i rgyud skor* (Ed. T. Tashi), *gter ma* rediscovered by Guru Nontse (Gu ru rnon rtse) in the eleventh century. Reproduced from original manuscript belonging to the Samling Monastery (bSam gling), in Dolpo, N.W. Nepal.

Sangpo, J. (Ed.) (1999). *The Four Collections of Nectar Treasures of Medicine Science (Gsi rig bdud rtsi'i bang mdzod 'bum bzhi)*. New Delhi, India: Paljor Publications.

Shardza, T.G. (1974a). (Shar rdza bkhra shis rgyal mtshan), Channels-Breaths Magical Movements of Oral Tradition [of Zhang Zhung]. In N. Sonam, S. T. Gyaltsen and K. Gyatso (Eds.), *The Great Treasury of the Ultra Profound Sky (Yang zab nam mkha' mdzod chen las Snyan brgyud rtsa rlung 'khrul 'khor bshugs so), I–III*, (pp. 321–46). New Thobgyal, India: Tibetan Bonpo Monastic Centre.

____________. (1974b). Mass of Fire Primordial Wisdom: Bringing into Experience the Common Inner Heat (*Thun mong gtum mo'i nyams len ye shes me dpung*). In Khedup Gyatso (Ed.), *The Self-Arising of the Three Buddha Bodies (Rdzogs pa chen po sku gsum rang shar)* (pp. 1–54). Delhi, India: Tibetan Bonpo Monastic Centre.

Servan-Schreiber, D. (2007). *Anticancer. A New Way of Life*. Paris, France: Robert Laffont (translation in English, UK: Penguin Books, 2008).

Wangyal, T. (2006). *Tibetan Sound Healing*. Boulder, Colorado: Sounds True.

____________. (2011). Awakening the Sacred Body, New York City, New York: Hay House.

A DEPICTION OF THE TIBETAN MIND: A RARE PORTRAIT OF THE ANCIENT BON MASTER TAPIHRITSA

John Vincent Bellezza

John Vincent Bellezza

Hidden away in western Tibet is an ancient rock painting of great cultural significance. This extremely unusual portrait depicts Tapihritsa (*Ta pi hri tsa*), the propagator of a tradition of personal cultivation that is central to the Bon religion. Perhaps the oldest known portrait of this hallowed figure still in existence, it embellishes the ruins of a hermitage nestled at the base of a towering rock escarpment. This long-abandoned place of retreat is known either as the Red-coloured Temple (*Lha khang dmar chag*) or Deer Face Temple (*Sha ba gdong lha khang*).

A partial view of the ancient Bon hermitage called either the Red-coloured Temple or Deer Face Temple, as the case may be. The portrait of the religious master Tapihritsa is out of view on the right side of the photograph. Note the red and white striped

façade in the foreground and the profuse assortment of Bon symbols and inscriptions scrawled on the shelter in the background.

Overlooking the limpid, turquoise waters of Darok Yumtso (*Da rog g.yu mtsho*), several brightly painted rock shelters of the Red-coloured Temple once housed individuals immersed in meditative practices believed to offer deep insight into the formation and character of the universe. According to the teachings of Tapihritsa and other great sages of his lineage, reality at its most fundamental level is comprised of the mind in its primal or pure luminous state. This understanding of the nature of existence was not restricted to great saints living in solitude. In fact, it had a profound influence on how Tibetans see the world and their place in it.

Until the 12th or 13th century, the Red-coloured Temple and other sacred sites at Lake Darok belonged to Bon, Tibet's indigenous religion. Traces of archaic temples and residences dot the north shore and two islands in the lake. Monuments associated with the Bon religion of more recent centuries are lacking at Lake Darok. This suggests that, by the 13th century, the region had been converted to Buddhism in the relentless spread of this religion across much of Tibet. The Red-coloured Temple has been abandoned ever since, a forlorn reminder of past religious glories. For the most part, Buddhist monks and meditators avoid ancient Bon sites at Lake Darok, perceiving them as haunted with the memories and spirits of the older religion.

The Red-coloured Temple and surrounding rock formations of many hues were ideal for contemplative pursuits. The desirability of the site was further enhanced by holy Lake Darok and its potable waters. According to the Bon sacred geographic tradition, Lake Darok is home to a beneficent goddess named Dayarse Mengodema (*Da yar se sman go de ma*). Originally a lake protectress of Zhang Zhung, she is the protector of Bon devotees and monks, as well as the countryside, domestic and wild animals, and subterranean treasures.

The rock painting of the Bon sage Tapihritsa, one of the oldest known artistic portrayals of this personality in Tibet. It is written that he was born into a shepherd's family in the kingdom of Zhang Zhung (his name is in the Zhang Zhung language).

The image of Tapihritsa at the Red-coloured Temple was identified as such by Bon's most senior scholar, the Ven. Lopon Tenzin Namdak. Lopon Tenzin Namdak was so kind as to re-examine photographs of the fresco in 2016, providing further comments. I first documented this rock painting in November 1997, on my first expedition to Lake Darok. Travelling on foot, I was directed to the lake's north side by local shepherds (*'brog pa*), who explained that there were many ancient Bon ruins there.

Situated on the eastern edge of the Red-coloured Temple, the image of Tapihritsa and accompanying mantras appear to have had a dedicatory function, identifying and legitimizing the religious lineage of his successors. The style of painting belongs unmistakably to the tradition of western Tibet, but it is the only fresco known in the entire region identifiable as Bon. The painting of Tapihritsa possesses major iconographical traits still associated with him in that religion; however, it also contains curious features not seen in the extant artistic tradition.

Painted in red and orange ochre and a calcareous white pigment, Tapihritsa's likeness is bold and elementary in form, ornamenting a huge expanse of otherwise unadorned rock. In making this depiction, a thick layer of clay and mud plaster was initially applied to the escarpment and carefully smoothed. Then, a thin veneer of fine clay was added over the base and polished. With the backing in place, the actual painting of the image could commence.

The outline or aureole around the figure of Tapihritsa consists of white and red lines drawn in parallel. His body was painted in white, with fine anatomical details like the eyes and hands outlined in a greyish pigment that seems to underlie the entire painting. Unfortunately, the fresco has been heavily damaged, precluding a detailed iconographic analysis of its aesthetic elements. In Bon texts, Tapihritsa is described as a translucent white figure devoid of clothing. While he is white-coloured in the Lake Darok rock painting, it is not clear that he is naked. Rather, he may possibly be cast as a bodhisattva, wearing garments and ornaments. In the fresco, as well as in more conventional Bon renditions, Tapihritsa's hands meet on his lap in a gesture of meditational equipoise.

The trilobate aureole, the stepped throne upon which the meditating figure sits, the prominent folded legs, and the palette suggest that it was painted circa 1050–1300. That was a period in which Buddhist fresco painting flourished in western Tibet, spreading to many temples, both parietal and freestanding.

Most of the Buddhist sites contemporaneous with the Red-coloured Temple were located in the extreme western Tibet and in Spiti and Ladakh, far from Lake Darok. From historical accounts, such as the *Royal Annals of Western Tibet* (*Mnga' ris rgyal rabs*) and the edicts of Lha Lama Yesheö (Lha bla ma ye shes 'od, 947–1024), we know that Buddhist elites moved to suppress Bon beliefs and customs beginning in the late 10th century. Far removed from the major population centres of the lower elevation western valleys, the Red-coloured Temple evidently persisted as a Bon place of worship because of its remoteness. Set on the high plateau or Changthang (*Byang thang*), it seems that Lake Darok largely escaped Buddhist missionary activities in the early second millennium.

Tapihritsa is thought to have lived in the 7th to 8th centuries, the 24th and final master of a prehistoric line known as the Oral Tradition of Zhangzhung (*Zhang zhung snyan rgyud*). This succession of saints transmitted a powerful system of mind training known as Dzogchen (*Rdzogs chen*). Dzogchen constitutes the highest teachings of Bon (also found in the Nyingmapa school of Tibetan Buddhism), a tradition that both encapsulates and supersedes all other doctrines of the faith. Tapihritsa is believed to have realized the natural state of the mind, the fabric of consciousness in which all things are wrapped. Simply put, this is a non-conceptual, non-dualistic state of being.

A child prodigy, Tapihritsa received the Dzogchen teachings from his father and other great masters. As part of his training, he spent nine years alone in the wilds of the Changthang, leading to both mundane and extraordinary attainments. He is said to have assumed the ultimate form of being or *bonku (bon sku)* in his lifetime and to have left the world in a rainbow body (*'ja' lus*), leaving no mortal traces behind.

The main student of Tapihritsa was Nangsher Lödpo (*Snang bzher lod po*), a highly adept Dzogchen master in his own right. In order to instruct this formidable figure, Tapihritsa appeared as a boy, humbling Nangsher Lödpo with his superior knowledge of the supreme path. According to Bon historical texts, Nangsher Lödpo went on to become the chief priest of the Tibetan emperor Trisong Deutsen (*Khri srong lde'u btsan*). This is supposed to have occurred after punishing King Trisong Deutsen for orchestrating the assassination of Likmigya (*Lig mi rgya*), the king of Zhangzhung. The exploits and teachings of Tapihritsa, Nangsher Lödpo and other great Dzogchen adepts are told in Bon scriptures such as the 14th century biographical text *Zhang zhung snyan rgyud bla ma'i rnam thar*, composed by Patön Tengyal Sangpo (*Spa ston bstan rgyal bzang po*). While very few Tibetans are accomplished Dzogchen practitioners, the conviction that reality is all-inclusive, transcending thought processes, permeates the faith of ordinary Tibetans still today.

The stucco panel with bichrome painting of Tapihritsa. Three Bon mantras are written below it in red ochre.

In addition to the painting of Tapihritsa, three Bon mantras were written in red ochre on the same stucco panel. The top line begins with the three seed syllables (*sa bon*) for meditative practice rendered in an obsolete style: *A Om hum*. The highly fragmentary lettering to the left of this mantra is no longer legible. In this spot, one might expect to find the eight-syllable *matri* mantra (*Om' ma tri mu ye sa le 'du*). This sacred ejaculation is held to purify the male and female principles and six realms of the universe and is written on the ruins of the Red-coloured Temple. To the right of the mantras on the first line is a swastika, one or more circles, three flaming jewels (*nor bu me 'bar*), and perhaps other sacred motifs now obscured. While these religious pictographs are of significant age, they seem to have been added to the panel after the creation of the Tapihritsa fresco and mantras. There is also much holy graffiti on the nearby rock shelters.

The second and third lines of the panel consist of a mantra attributed to the founder of Bon, Shenrab Miwo (*Gshen rab mi bo*), which is dedicated to the primordial Buddha Kuntusangpo (*Kun tu bzang po*). It reads: *"A' A dkar sa le 'od A yang Om' 'du. A dkar A rmad du tri su nag po zhi mal"*.

Although the painting and epigraphy of the Red-coloured Temple are as much as a thousand years old, they are instantly recognizable in the Bon religious milieu of today. This unique monument and art help corroborate historical accounts concerning the primary role of the Changthang in the dissemination of Bon Dzogchen practices. The fresco of Tapihritsa, made some three to five hundred years after he is supposed to have disappeared into the sky, goes some distance in establishing the historicity of this noble personage. At the very least it shows that he was indeed known to Bon practitioners in western Tibet prior to the codification of texts for the Oral Tradition of Zhangzhung.

MENDRUB OSER KYILPA: THE LIGHT INFUSED MEDICINE BLESSING RITUAL

Collin Millard

Collin Millard, PhD

My aim here is to give a brief outline of the Bon *mendrub* ritual known as *Dutsi Oser Kyilpa* ("the light infused nectar"). There are numerous types of *mendrub* rituals found in the Bon religion, as well as in the four main sects of Tibetan Buddhism, but the *Dutsi Oser Kyilpa* ritual, due to its high prestige, long duration, high elaboration, rarity, and expense, stands in a class of its own. I have had the good fortune to witness the ritual on two occasions, at the Triten Norbutse Bon monastery in Kathmandu. The first time was in January 1998, and the second time was in December 2012. The ritual involves months of preparation and takes two weeks to perform.

In addition to the monks living in the monastery, on both occasions a few hundred people attended the ritual from Bon communities in Kathmandu, Mustang, Dhorpatan and Dolpo. Most of them were lay people. Around 20 Bon *nagpa* (householder priests) from Dolpo and Lubrag also attended the ritual on both occasions. The main ritual activities were undertaken by 32 monks. However, all the people present were participants, as each person had some role to play. In 1998, only a handful of westerners were present. In 2012, around 100 western students attended the ritual from numerous countries.

In 1998, for the three weeks prior to the ritual, I worked with Khenpo Tenpa Yungrung to translate the main guide book of the ritual, written by the Bon lama Tsultrim Gyaltsen. He lived in the 14th century, at the time of the Bon monastery Yeru Wensaka. He was a famous Bon scholar and wrote many texts, including important works on cosmogony. The *yidam* of the ritual is Shitro (*zhi khro*). This is a composite name made up of two parts, a peaceful and a wrathful aspect represented by the peaceful deity, Shiwa, and the wrathful deity, Trowo. All *yidam* have these two aspects, but in the Bon tradition, Shitro refers to a distinct *yidam*, one of the five *yidam* of the father tantras. The peaceful form of the *yidam* represents the *dharmakaya*. The wrathful form of the *yidam* represents the *sambhogakaya* and the *nirmanakaya*. The full name of the peaceful deity is Shiwa Yungdrung Yong Dzog (*zhi ba gyung drung yongs rdzogs*), and that of the wrathful deity is Trowo Tsochog Khagying (*khro bo gtso mchog mkha' 'gying*), but the latter is most often referred to simply as Tsochog. Shitro is also the principal Bon deity connected with the practice of achieving liberation in the intermediate state after death (*bar do thos grol*). Shiwa emanates 45 peaceful deities and Trowo emanates 86 wrathful deities; these are all related to the five Buddha families. Through meditative practice, we can develop the capacity to perceive these deities at different stages of the death process. If we do not develop this ability, the deities will appear through our impure deluded vision as demons chopping up and devouring our bodies. The ritual then is based on three texts, the Mendrub Oser Kyilpa text, the ritual guide book, and the texts of Shiwa and Trowo. During the ritual, prayers and mantras are recited from relevant section of all three texts

TROWO TSOCHOG KHAGYING AND THE 86 WRATHFUL DEITIES

The purpose of the ritual is to transform a medicinal powder containing 120 ingredients into a powerful medicine capable of curing the 400 classes of disease spoken about in Tibetan medicine. The medicines are transformed through a tantric process that has corresponding effects on the minds of the participants; alongside the transformation of the raw medicinal compound into a healing nectar, the five mental poisons present in the minds of the participants are transformed into associated transcendental wisdoms and thereby each participant is led to an awareness of their own enlightened nature.

RITUAL ACTIVITIES

The Oser Kyilpa ritual text is divided into three parts. The first two parts deal with the elements of the ritual. The third part concerns the purpose and achievements of the practice.

1. PRELIMINARY ACTIVITIES

The first part consists of three groups of preliminary activities. The first group of preliminary activities is the outer preliminaries. These are concerned with finding a qualified lama, and the gathering of qualified individuals at a suitable location. The second group of preliminary activities is the inner preliminaries. These involve collecting all the items needed for the ritual and then ritually purifying them along with the medicinal ingredients, offerings and food for the participants.

The guide book explains that there are three different groups of ritual implements to be gathered: general ritual implements, ritual implements for the practitioner, and ritual implements for the deities. The guide book explains that all the necessary objects should be gathered for the mandala, such as the pots to contain the medicines and so on. Also listed in this section is the need to find the right building to carry out the practice. A further element described here is the need to prepare the *lingka (ling ga)*. This is an effigy which is used during the ritual to destroy all obstacles. The effigy is made in the likeness of a person. The practitioners visualise that all obstructors are dissolved into the effigy and then it is destroyed. The obstructors can be anything that obstructs one's path. It is said that there are 80,000 types of obstructers.

DESTROYING OBSTACLES BY OFFERING AND EFFIGY

At this stage, various offerings are made to the local deities and obstructors. One of these offerings is ser *kyem*. This is *chang* containing a piece of gold as a mark of respect. This was traditionally done in Tibet for people of high status. In the context of the ritual, it is offered to the *sadag*, the spirit owner of the land. This is a way of asking permission from the *sadag* to use the land to perform the ritual. This needs to be done, otherwise there could be disturbances to the ritual.

The next part of the ritual involves purifying the ritual space. The procedures involved in this part of the ritual are complex and require a good understanding of Tibetan astrology. There are many different types of *sadag*. According to Tibetan astrology, there is a daily *sadag* cycle which involves 12 changes. There are also major changes in the *sadag* cycle throughout the year. The *sadag* ritual also depends on whether the ritual has been done before at the location or if it is the first time.

This *sadag* is present in the earth. He is considered to be lying down in the earth. His head moves according to the yearly progression of the 12 animals in Tibetan astrology. His head faces the direction of the predominating seasonal animal, with his tail in the opposite direction. For example, at the time of the year when the tiger is predominant, the *sadag's* head will be pointing east. By taking into account this yearly cycle, one can calculate the exact location at any given time of the *sadag's* stomach. The earth that is needed for the ritual can be taken from there. By digging in that location, one digs into the fat of *sadag's* stomach, and this will not cause harm to the *sadag*. During the ritual, the monks walk in a ceremonial line and take earth from the chosen location. This is then taken inside the temple for the mandala.

EARTH TAKEN FROM THE *SADAG'S* STOMACH

The next section of the ritual involves gathering and assembling the material necessary to create a barrier around the ritual site. The barrier has two elements. The first part involves setting up a series of ritual spears called *wal dung (dbal mdung)*. "Dung" simply means "spear." "Wal" is a Zhang Zhung word; one of its meanings is "sharp," but on another level, the word refers to the wrathful deities.

RITUAL SPEARS

The second part involves preparing pictures of the four protector deities that will be set up at each of the cardinal points:

East – the protector *shar mi dkar seng ge,* who has a white human body with the head of a mountain lion.

North – the protector *byang mi dmar phag,* who has a red human body with a pig's head.

West – the protector *nub mi sngon 'brug,* who has a blue human body with a dragon's head.

South – the protector *lho mi nag dom,* who has a black human body with a bear's head.

Fours Protectors

Southern Protector

The setting up of the four protectors marks the beginning of the third and final set of preliminary practices. The rest of the preliminary practices concern constructing the mandala and setting up the ritual objects and medicines at the relevant locations on the mandala. There are two classes of objects that are placed on the mandala. The first group of objects includes a range of ritual items that are common to all tantric practice, including ritual daggers (*phur ba*) and ritual claws (*spar shad*). An umbrella-like object (*gla gur*) is set above the mandala. The usual procedure for tantric ritual is that relevant prayers are recited as the objects are placed on each section of the mandala. However, in the Mendrub ritual, all the prayers are recited together at the end.

Having gathered all the necessary objects, the practitioners establish the four protectors at each of the cardinal points and offer *ser kyem* to them and ask them to stop all obstructors coming in and any accomplishments getting out. During the ritual, three boundaries are established to prevent the harmful effects of obstructors. This marks the outer boundary. Later in the ritual, a middle and an inner boundary will be established.

The Mandala of Shiwa

Medicine Pots and Ritual Implements on the Mandala

The second group of objects are the special objects which are specific to the Mendrub Oser Kyilpa ritual; that is to say the pots containing the medicinal ingredients. These are brought to the mandala by clean boys and girls, as required by the main text. The practitioners then invite the nectar to the medicine. They do this by reciting prayers and mantras and making downward waving movements with ritual arrows, bells and drums in a gesture of invitation. In this fashion, they "escort" the young boys and girls carrying the medicine pots.

The medicines are divided into main and subsidiary medicines. There are five groups of main medicines connected with the five elements, five Buddha families, five mental poisons and five transcendental wisdoms. Each of the five main groups includes certain medicinal plants used in Tibetan medicines and several special medicines, such as "the sperm of a lion," "the stool of a horse with a blue mane and tail, collected while it is running," "blood of red birds," and so on. These ingredients are put in pots made of specific materials and placed on the cardinal points and centre of the mandala. The subsidiary medicines, which the text associates with the 8 forms of consciousness, are put in agate pots and placed on the mid points of the mandala. Through the ritual, these 8 forms of consciousness are to be realised as the 8 deities of the natural state of the mind.

Then the pots are placed on the mandala in the following sequence:

1st – the glass pot is placed at the centre of the mandala (Space / Mind Buddha Family)

2nd – the gold pot is placed in the east of the mandala (Earth / Body Buddha Family)

3rd – the turquoise pot is place in the north of the mandala (Air / Knowledge Buddha Family)

4th – the copper pot is placed in the west of the mandala (Fire / Speech Buddha Family)

5th – the iron pot is placed in the south of the mandala (Water / Activity Buddha Family)

6th – the four agate pots are placed at the mid-directions

The preliminary section of the ritual concludes with the door of the mandala being ritually opened and the participants taking the necessary tantric vows and commitments, and each receiving a secret name.

Yogzin Tenzin Namdag Giving the Empowerment

2. THE MAIN ACTIVITIES

The main activities of the ritual are divided into three parts:

1. Blessing the raw medicines
2. Blessing the medicinal powders
3. Bestowing the empowerment and accomplishments

During the ritual, there were a number of locations where ritual activity took place. The main activity occurred inside the temple, where the mandala was located. In a large room near the temple, the monks who were not taking part in the main ritual activities collectively recited ritual texts throughout the ritual. In another room, a group of Bon *nagpas* from Dolpo and Lubrag recited another group of texts. Meanwhile, people circumambulated the main temple, reciting the Oser *kyilpa* mantra around the clock, every day. First the raw medicines are consecrated on the mandala of the peaceful deity and then on the mandala of the wrathful deity. The same procedure is then performed for the powdered medicines. The main activities culminate with the tantric empowerments of Shiwa and Trowo.

3. FRUIT AND PURPOSE OF THE PRACTICE

The Purpose of the Practice

1. To realise one's Buddha nature outside the cycles of death and rebirth

2. To fulfil the mind of the deities of emptiness

3. To eliminate the 400 classes of disease. To transform the 80,000 demons of affliction into forces of good and to transform into wisdom the five main demons of *samsara* associated with the negative mental dispositions of anger, desire, ignorance, jealousy and pride.

The Fruits of the Practice

The following benefits will arise from the practice:

1. The practice enables one to realise the nature of mind.

2. The demon of ignorance will be transformed into the wisdom which understands the true nature of emptiness.

3. One's understanding of the nature of mind will be persistent and unwavering, like a victory banner held high in the sky.

4. The roots of the medicines and the *samsaric* passions of the practitioner will be transformed into wisdom, and the lamp of clarity and compassion will be raised.

5. The branches of the medicines will be transformed into bliss and one's impure understanding of phenomenon will transform

into the vision of all as having a blissful nature. The devil of old age and degeneration will be transformed into unchangeable, undying nature, symbolised by the Bonpo Yungdrung Swastika.

6. The leavcs of the medicines will be transformed into nectar, the devil of death into a source of unceasing life, and the life force of the Yungdrung Swastika will be sustained.

7. The world and all sentient beings within it will be transformed into fundamental perfection.

8. The demons that beguile the practitioners with miraculous illusory forms will dissolve into the unborn empty nature of all phenomena and the flag of wisdom beyond conception will be hoisted.

9. The practice of *mendrub* is like a wish-fulfilling jewel where whatever one wishes will be fulfilled. Through it, one's spiritual practice will become fruitful and one will achieve the common and supreme attainments. The text says that the practitioner will become like a great emperor and will pass beyond the clutches of death and rebirth.

dbal gsas thun lung gi dkyil 'khor
Mandala of the Fierce Deity Thunlung
Acrylic and mineral color on canvas
67 x 67 cm
2013

དཔལ་གསས་སྔགས་ཞི་ག་ཆེན་གྱི་དཀྱིལ་འཁོར།

ACKNOWLEDGMENTS

The Enlightened Vision Association (EVA) was born out of the desire to contribute to the preservation of the Himalayan heritage and cultural values within and beyond the Himalayan region. EVA is a not-for-profit, non-governmental and non-denominational association based in Geneva, Switzerland.

EVA supports local projects in the Himalayas by promoting Himalayan knowledge and traditional practices. EVA is also committed to making these known beyond the Himalayan borders by organising cultural events in Switzerland and in other European countries. For more information about our projects and event, please visit our website at www.evaassociation.org.

We would like to convey our deepest appreciation to the authors of the articles included in this book, as well as to those who supported its creation, including Sonia Rollinet, Matias Perez Toscani, Joanne Massoubre, Micheline Hossain, David and Uma Mishra Newbery, Arch I platform and EVA's partners Sherig Phuntsok Ling Bon Society, Architecture & Development France, Yungdrung Bon Stiftung Germany, L'Association AOM/ AOM YOGA Switzerland, KSS YCom Bern and the Coopérative sociale et culturelle Immunitas Switzerland.

Our thanks also go to other talented and generous photographers for their photographs featured in this book: Jack Brauer for donating the photograph entitled "Ama Dablam Alpenglow Reflection" from the Khumbu region of Nepal (www.MountainPhotography.com) featured in pages 134-135; Shreeram M. V. for the photograph "Pangong Tso Magic" featured on pages 94-95 (www.darter.

in); Berta Tilmantaitė for the photograph on pages 100-101 (http://godoberta.com/project/himalaya/).

We are equally grateful to the Bel-Air Fine Art Gallery in Geneva and to François Chabanian for hosting the exhibition "Mandalas, Mirrors of the Cosmos" in 2013, and to the organisers of the second edition of the exhibition at Espace Lhomond in Paris in 2014.

Thanks to Max Kolpak and Gina Ilie for the design of this book and to Jo Lavender for proofreading it.

Our deepest appreciation goes to Khenpo Tenpa Yungdrung Rinpoche for his essential contribution to the Mandalas' exhibitions and for his tireless work for the TISE Himalayan International School.

All proceeds from the Mandalas' exhibitions and from this book go to the TISE Himalayan International School in Siliguri, India. THIS aims at providing children from the Himalayan region with a modern education that takes into account their cultural heritage and traditional values.

Tise is the Tibetan term for Mount Kailash, an essential feature of Himalayan culture.

TO SUPPORT THIS AND OTHER EVA PROJECTS, WE WELCOME YOUR DONATIONS AT:

Enlightened Vision Association (EVA)
PostFinance – Contact Center
Mingerstrasse 20
CH-3030 Berne, Switzerland
Bank account number: 12-314841-7
IBAN: CH280900 0000 1231 4841 7
BIC: POFICHBEXXX
ISBN 978-2-940710-00-3

ENLIGHTENED VISION ASSOCIATION (EVA)

2021
Cuco Azul Books
Geneva, Switzerland

Printed in the USA
CPSIA information can be obtained
at www.ICGtesting.com
LVHW061827180923
758529LV00007B/107

THE LEGEND OF
ZELDA
Symphony OF THE Goddesses

Produced by
Alfred Music
P.O. Box 10003
Van Nuys, CA 91410-0003
alfred.com

Printed in USA.

ISBN-10: 1-4706-2629-2
ISBN-13: 978-1-4706-2629-7

THE LEGEND OF ZELDA
Symphony OF THE Goddesses

Contents

Movement I: The Ocarina of Time

Music by
KOJI KONDO

21
25
fp
fff
f
29
Zelda's Lullaby:
33
37
41

8va
46
ff
rit.
mp
51
(♩ = 80)
Great Deku Tree:
p
mp
55
59
p
pp
64
(♩ = 65)
Title Theme:
mp
sim.

68
72
76
mf
80
84
f

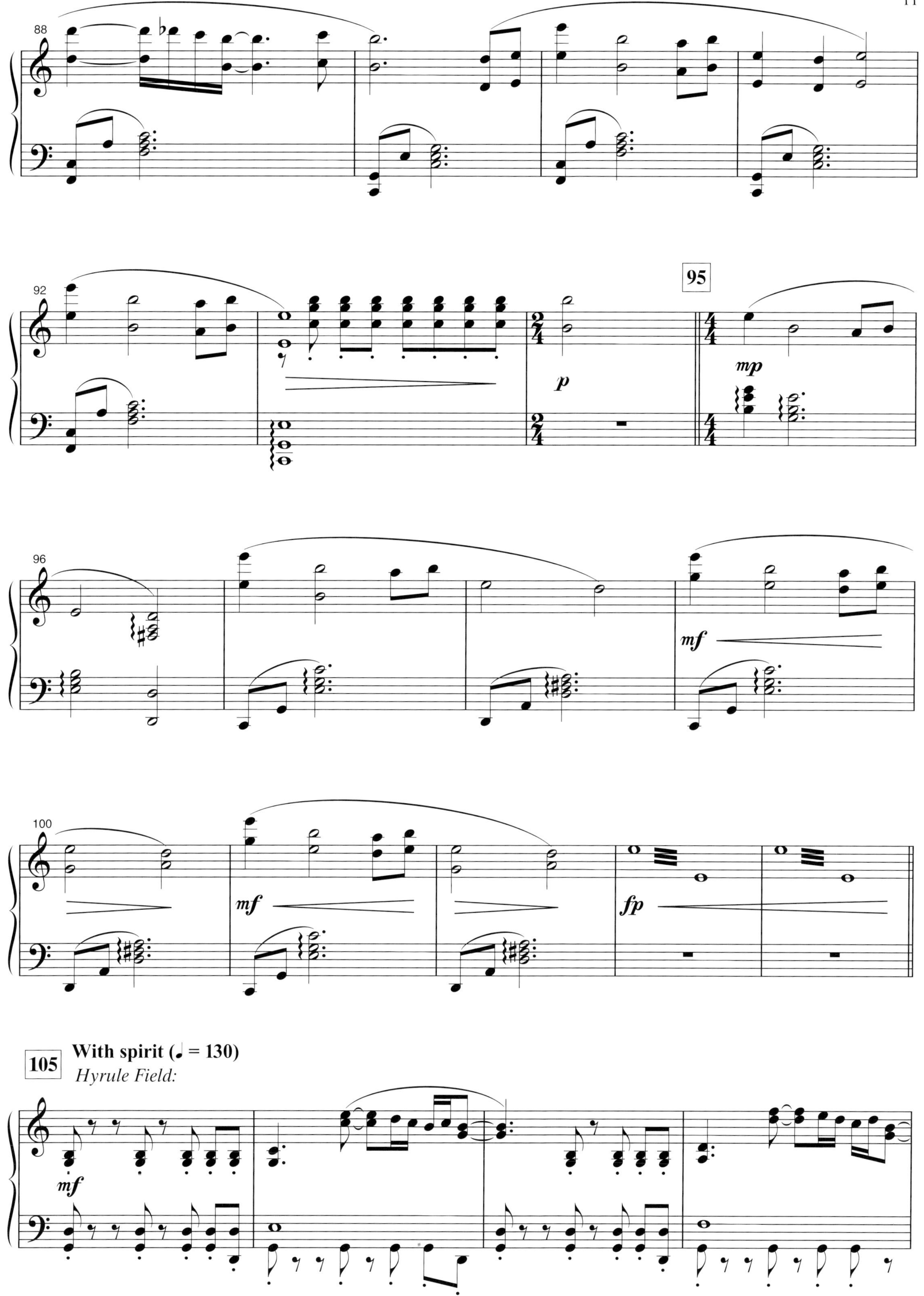
88
92
95
p
mp
96
mf
100
mf
fp
105
With spirit (♩ = 130)
Hyrule Field:
mf

109
113
3
7
f
117
121
125
129

133
137
141
mp
145
149
153

157
160
Gently (♩ = 70)
Sheik:
mp
161
165
169
173
rit.
174
(♩ = 60)
p
177

181
185
molto rit.
mp
p
190
Brightly (𝅗𝅥 = 190)
Ganondorf's Theme:
p
194
mp
198
f
ff

203
Ganondorf Battle:
f
206
209
212
215
218
ff
219
mf

221
224
227
229
mp
230
233
236
cresc.
f

239
242
245
248
251
8vb

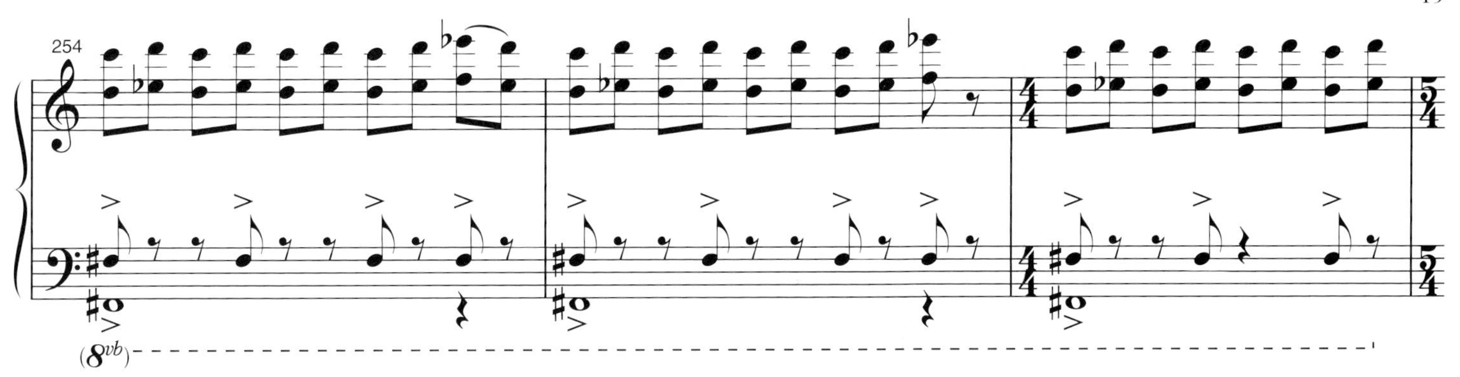
254
(8vb)

257

260

263
265
8vb

267
8va
mp

279 *Final Battle Beast Form:*

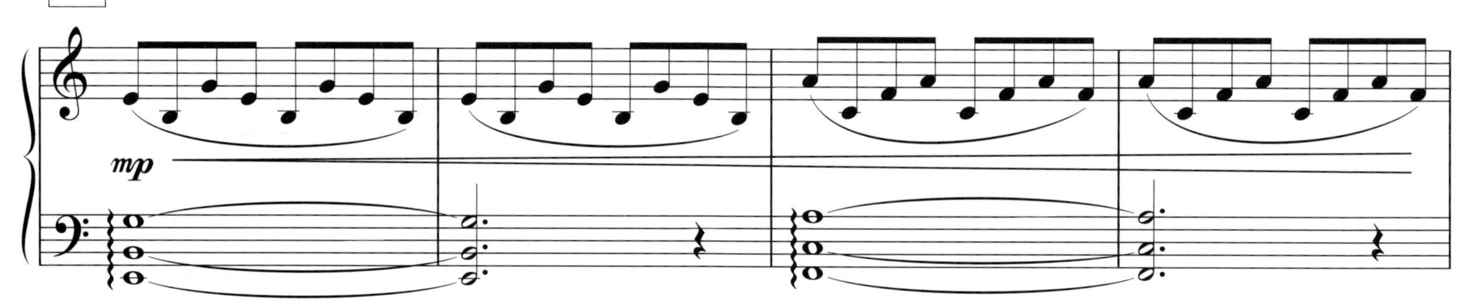

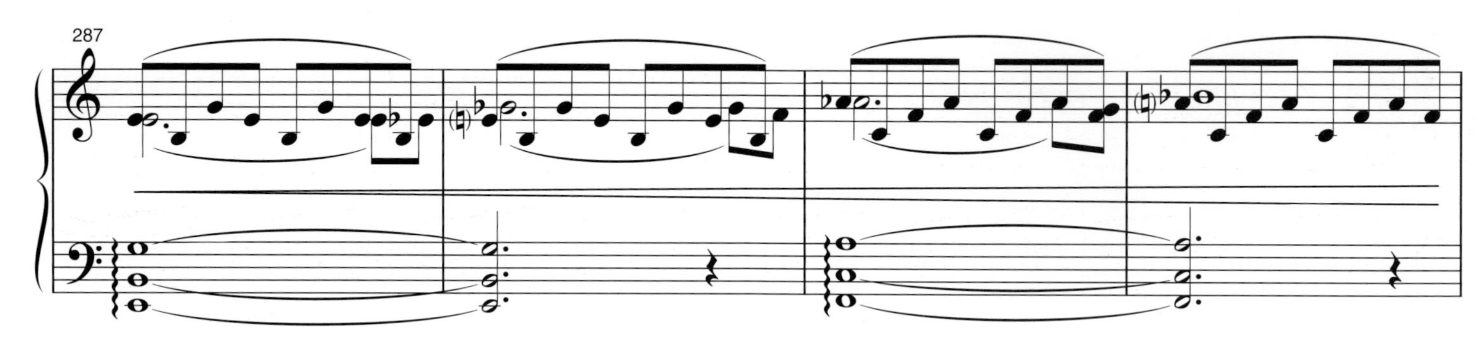

291
f
mf
295
mp
299
303
f
307
mp

311
f
315
319
f
ff
323
7
327

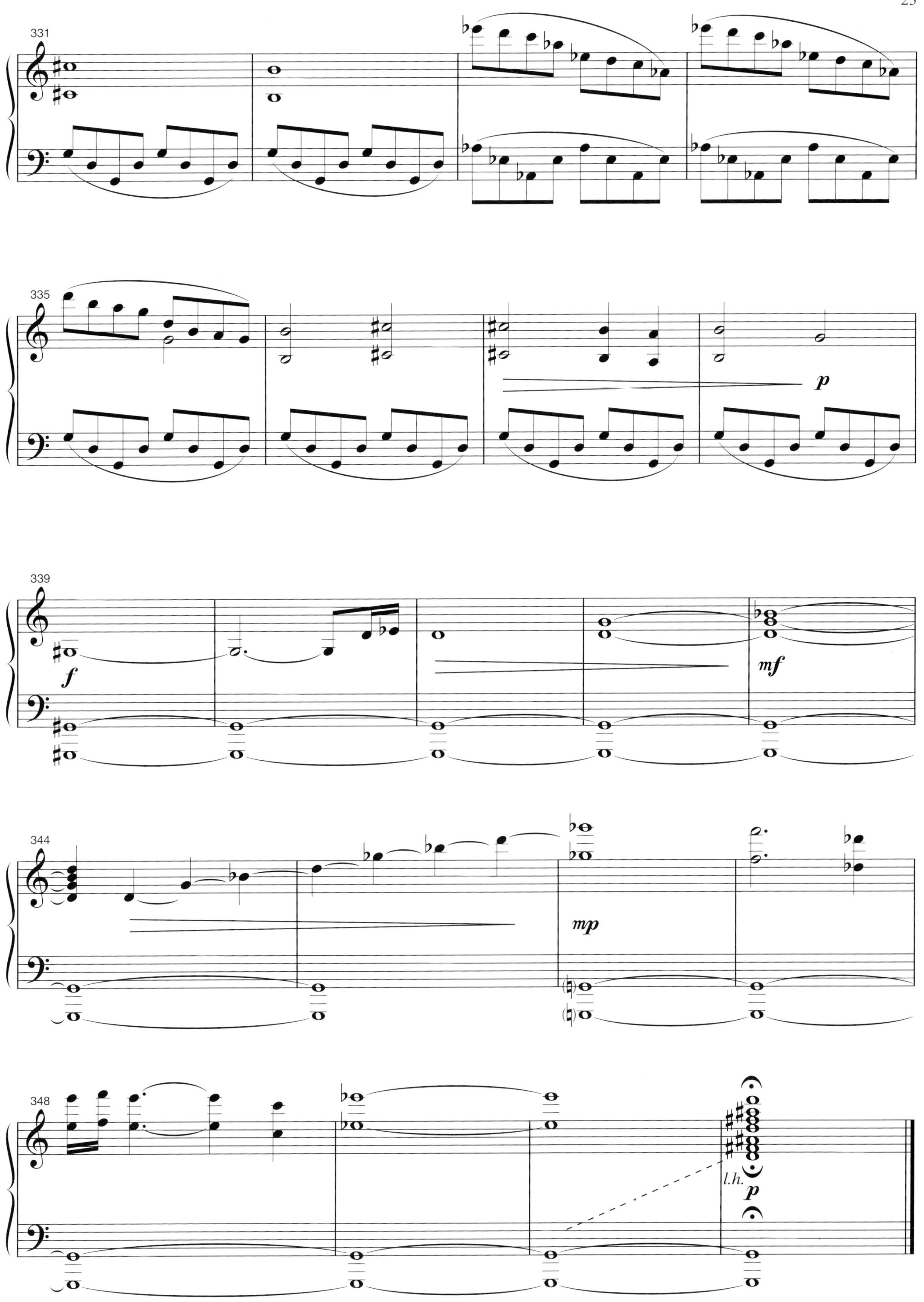
331
335
p
339
f
mf
344
mp
348
l.h.
p

Movement II: The Wind Waker

Music by
KENTA NAGATA, HAJIME WAKAI,
TORU MINEGISHI, and KOJI KONDO

17
Faster (♩ = 120)
Outset Island:
mf
21
25
29
33

37
41
45
49
53
3

56
59
Ocean:
mp
63
67
f
71

75
Slightly faster (♩ = 130)
78
82
Slower (♩ = 100)
86
Pirate Ship Theme:
mp
89

93
96
100
104
108

Aryll's Theme:
112
mf
117
accel.

Much faster (♩ = 150)
121
Aryll's Kidnapping:
f
fp
f

125

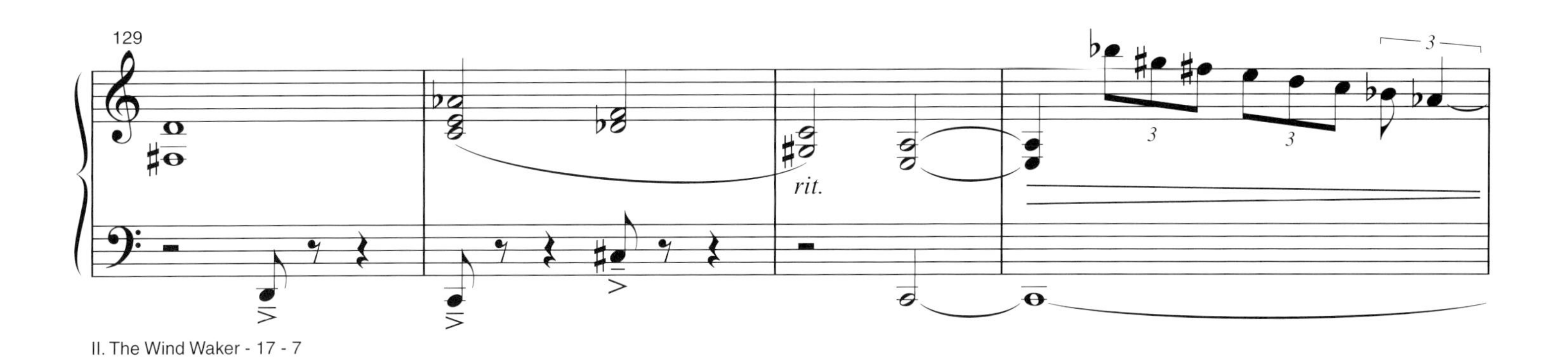
129
rit.

A little slower (♩ = 140)
135
Ocean continues:
133
mp
f
137
141
143
145
149
3

153
157
161
165
169
171
mp
f

173
mp
f
mp
f
177
mp
f
rit.
Much slower (♩ = 80)
180
Zelda's Awakening:
ff
181
Zelda Main Theme:
185
mp
3
189
sfz

193
Hero of the Wind:
f
3
196
199
202
205

Fast (♩ = 160)
208
ff
Ganondorf Battle Theme:
211
7
mp
ff
215
218
222

226
230
234
238
242

246
249
251
252
255
mp
259
mf

263
f

267
ff
fff

271
Slower, moderately (♩. = 120)
pp

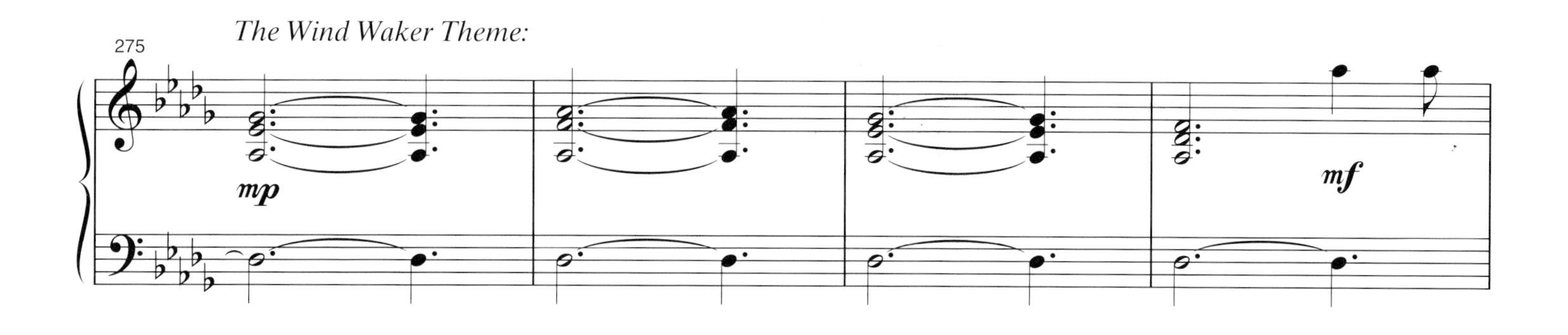
The Wind Waker Theme:
275
mp
mf

279

283
287
291
f
295
299

303
ff
307
311
4
315
318
fff

Movement III: The Twilight Princess

Music by
TORU MINEGISHI, ASUKA OHTA,
and KOJI KONDO

Faster (♩ = 80)
20 Light Spirit:

30
cresc.
mp
34
f
38
mp
42
43
Slower (𝅗𝅥. = 60)
Midna's Theme:
rall.
mp
46
mf

50
mp
53
55
57
58
Moderately bright (♩ =135)
Hyrule Field:
f
60
Di
Si
Ka
Di
Si
Ka.
ff

63
f
66
3
3
69
3
72
75
3
ff

77
80
cresc.
83
86
fff
mp
89

92
mf
96
99
102
A - sa - toh ma A - sa - toh - ma Sa - ta - may - ya Sa - ta - may - ya
ff
106
Toy - tha - sa - ha Toy - tha - sa - ha My - ri - thor - ma My - ri - thor - ma

110
A - sa - toh ma A - sa - toh - ma Sa - ta - may - ya Sa - ta - may - ya
114
Toy - tha - sa - ha Toy - tha - sa - ha My - ri - thor - ma My - ri - thor - ma
118 Excerpt from Main Theme:
f
3
3
122
126
ff

130
3
3

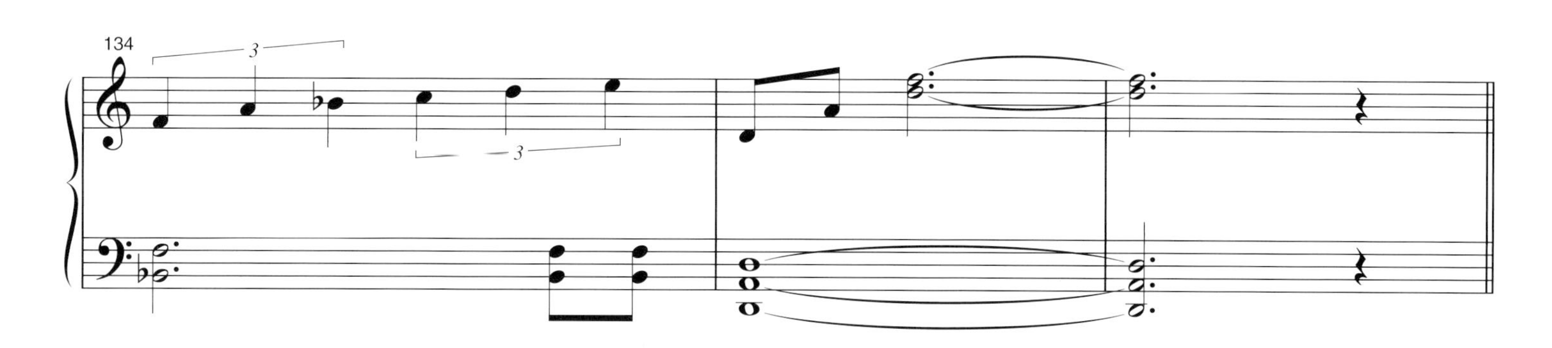
134
3
3

137
Slowly (♩. = 65)
The Sages' Theme:
f

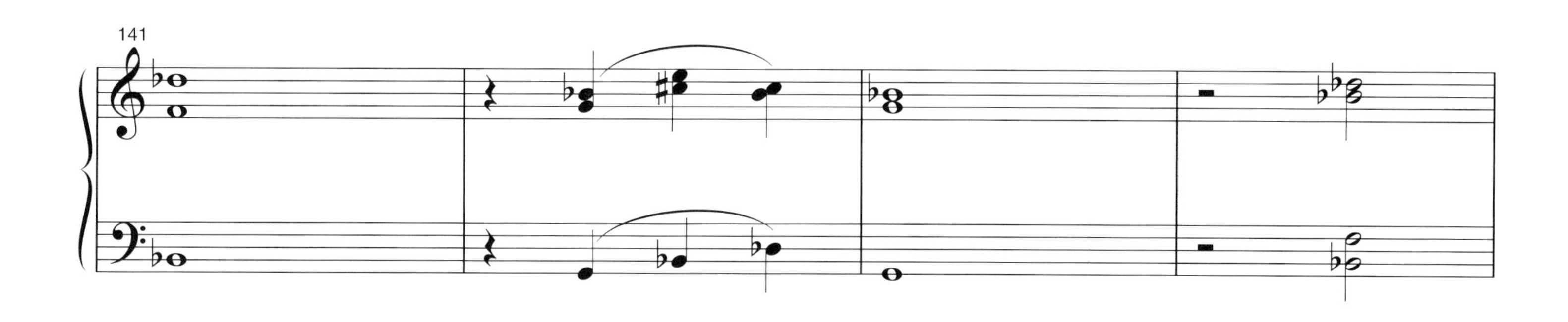
141

145

149
ff
mp
154
f
ff
accel.
159 Faster (♩ = 95)
Final Battle with Ganondorf:

163

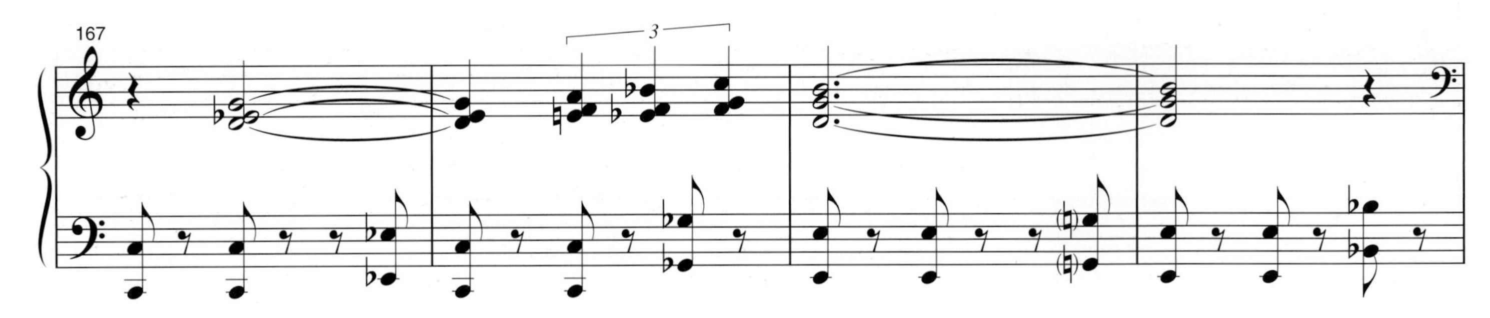
167

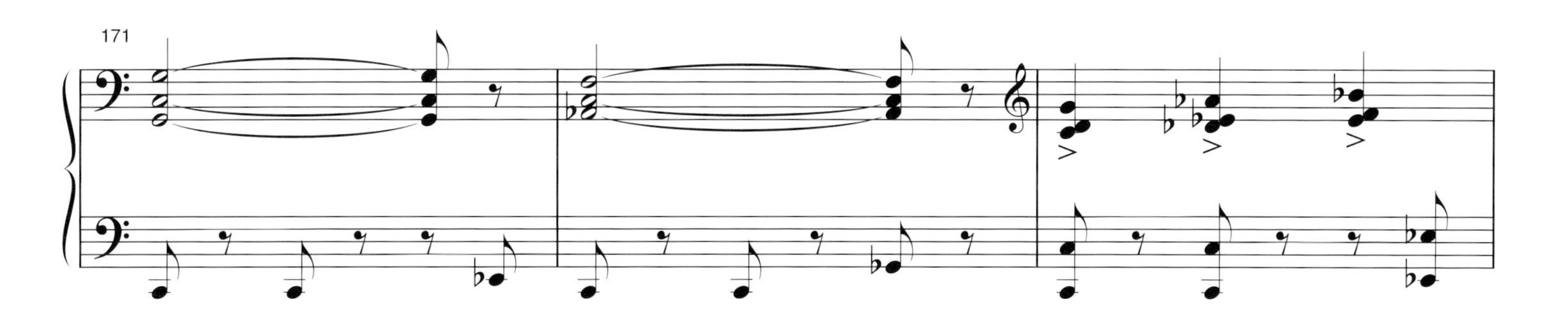
171

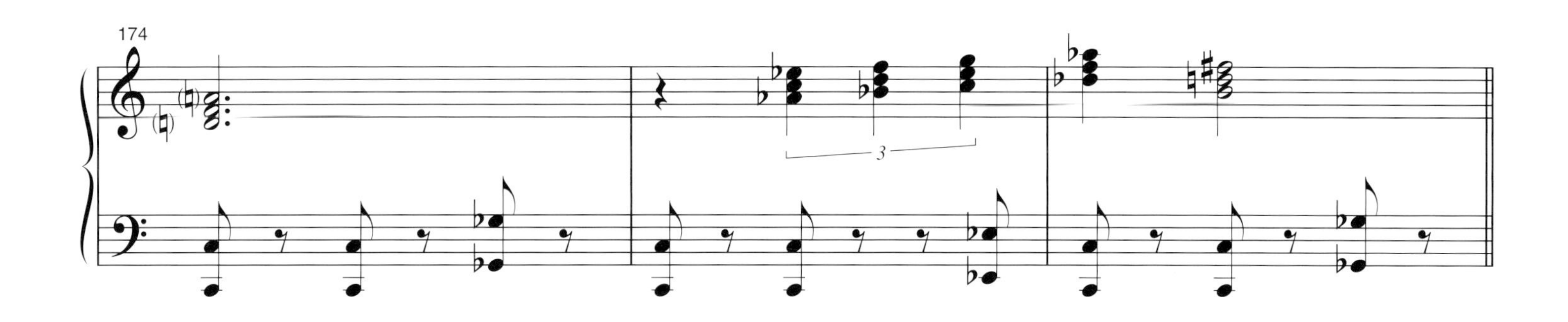
174

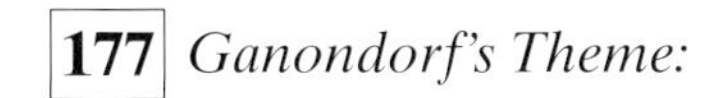
177 Ganondorf's Theme:

Sa Kree
Te Dak
Sa Kree
Te Dak
8vb

181
Sa Kree
Te Dak
Sa Kree
Te Dak
8vb

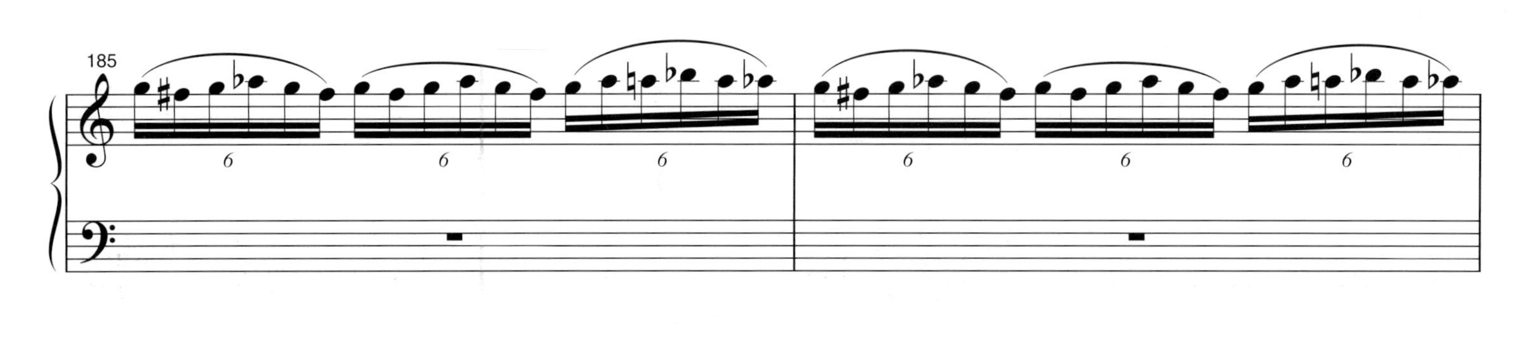
185
6
6
6
6
6
6

187
Ah
Ah
6
6
6
6
6
6

189
Ah
Ah
6
6
6
6
6
6

191
Ah
Ah
6
6
6
6
6
6

193
Ah
Ah
6
195
3
ff
199
Slower (♩ = 70)
Theme:
mp
202
205
accel.
cresc.

208
molto rit.
213
Zelda's Lullaby:
mp a tempo
217
221

225

229
232
Excerpt from Main Theme:
3
ff
p
235
f
ff
238
241
mp

Movement IV:
Time of the Falling Rain

Music by
KOJI KONDO

19
mf
f
23
27 Hyrule Castle:
p
31
mp
p
34
37
39
mf

40
44
47
p
mp
51
mf
f
pp
55
mp
58

61
63
67
71
74
77
Moderately slow (♩ = 85)
subito
rit.

81
Princess Zelda's Rescue:
p
(with pedal)
85
mp
89
93
97
101
mf

105
109
mp
113
mf
117
Excerpt from Legend of Zelda Theme:
p
121
mp
125

128
Moderately fast (♩. = 130)
(Cluster in different directions)
(Widen vibrato)
p
ff
8va
pp
mp
mf
131
ff
f
134
Men:
Sha ta sha ka ta
Sha ta sha ka ta
Sha ta sha ka ta
137
Sha ta sha ka ta
Sha ta sha ka ta
Sha ta sha ka ta

Full Choir:
140
Sha ta sha ka ta
Sha ta sha ka ta
Sha ta sha ka ta
143
Sha ta sha ka ta
Sha ta sha ka ta
Sha ta sha ka ta
146
Sha ta sha ka ta
Sha ta sha ka ta
Sha ta sha ka ta
149
Sha ta sha ka ta

152
Si
ka
Pa
di
156
Kro
ma
Ti
kay
mf
159
Dark World:
p
162
mp
166
mf

170
173
176
178
179
182
185

188
191
mf
194
197
199
202
mp

205 Dark Mountain Forest:
208
211
mf
213 Battle with Ganon:
mp
p
216
219

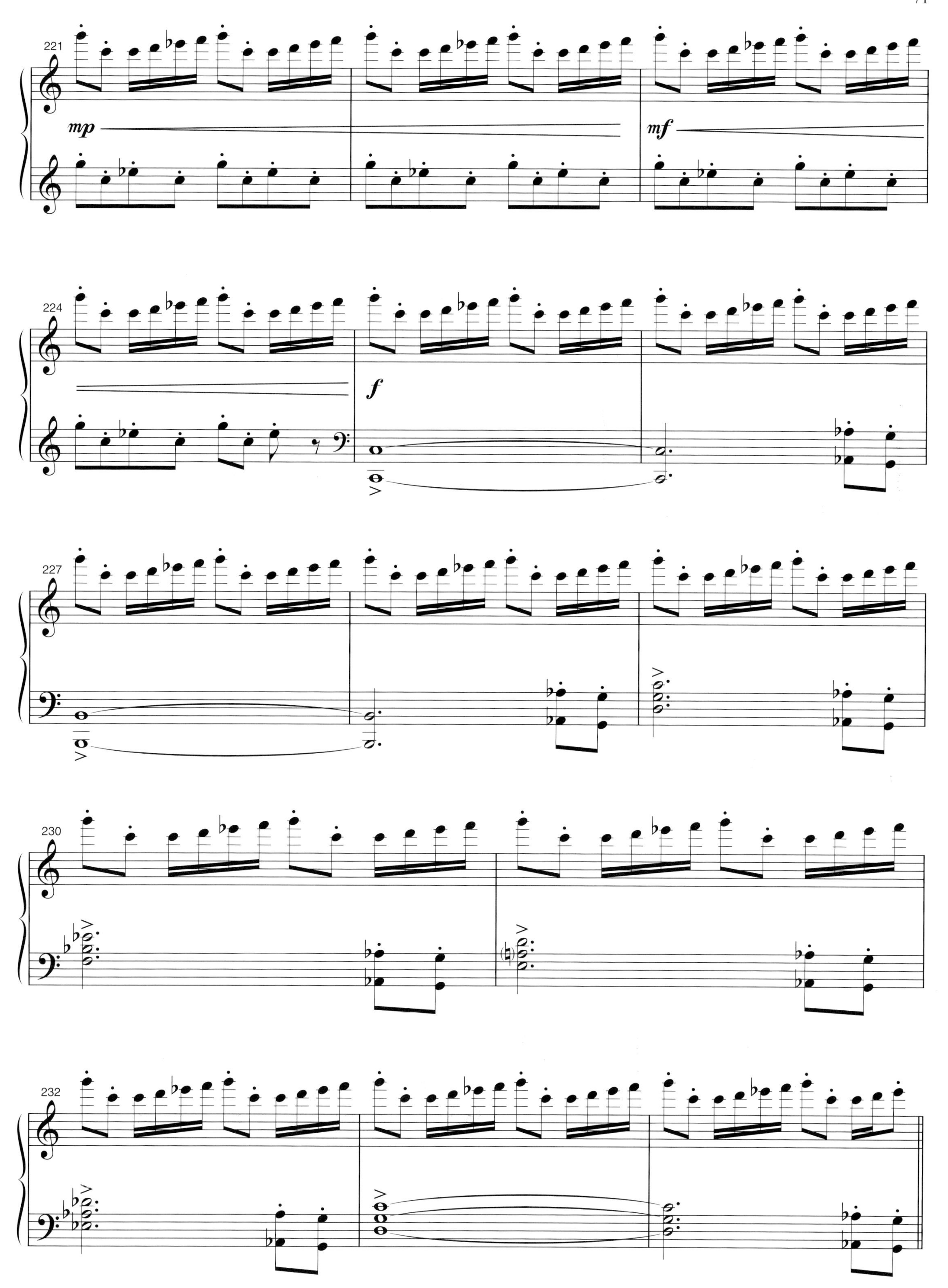
221
mp
mf
224
f
227
230
232

235
Ta vo
Cri vos
Sac tis
Ky-ri
239
Cri us
Ee nah
Vo tis
242
Si ka neh ta le pa dee fa Si ka neh ta le pa dee fa
mf
246
f
3

250
254
mp
257
rit.
Slowly (♩. = 65)
260
p
263
266
Triforce Chamber:

270
274
mp
278
282
286
mf

290
293
Moderately fast (♩ = 130)
296
300
Overworld/Legend of Zelda Theme:
Sa ki
Teh da
Sa ki
Teh da
304

308
311
mf
314
317
320
Ah.
f

323
ah
ah.
326
Ah
328
ah
331
ah
ah.

334
Ah
ah
338
ah
ah
341
ah.
Moderately fast (♩ = 100)
344
Ah
mf
f

347
ah
ah
350
ah
ah
ah
mf
354
ah
ah.
f
357
8vb